JAN

Every time I make a movie, everybody says it's the most expensive film in the film industry.

James Cameron, quoted in *Premiere*, December 1997

From *Aliens* to *Titanic*, James Cameron's films have spanned genres, broken box-office records, cleaned up at the Oscars, turned body-builders into movie stars and women into acceptable action heroes. Despite Cameron's undeniable influence on the high-concept postmodern blockbuster that dominated the 1980s and 1990s, there has until recently been little academic attention to his work.

Alexandra Keller provides the first critical study of James Cameron as "auteur", considering how his very presence in the cinematic landscape has changed the meaning of that term. Considering in particular his treatment of genre and gender, and his preoccupation with capital and vision itself, both in his films and in his filmmaking practice, Keller offers an overview of Cameron's work and its significance within cinematic history.

This study features a detailed overview of his films and career that situates Cameron in the larger context of contemporary popular culture, a critical review of the literature (both popular and academic) on Cameron and his films, and an in-depth analysis of Cameron's visual style across his feature fiction films. The book also includes a detailed chronology, filmography and extensive bibliography (including Internet resources).

Alexandra Keller is Assistant Professor of Film Studies at Smith College, Northampton, Massachusetts.

Routledge Film Guidebooks

The Routledge Film Guidebooks offer a clear introduction and overview of the work of key filmmakers, schools or movements. Each guidebook contains an introduction, including a brief history, defining characteristics and major films; a chronology; key debates surrounding the filmmaker or movement; and pivotal scenes, focusing on narrative structure, camera work and production quality.

Bollywood: a Guidebook to Popular Hindi Cinema
Tejaswini Ganti

Jane Campion
Deb Verhoeven

James Cameron
Alexandra Keller

JAMES CAMERON

ALEXANDRA KELLER

Routledge
Taylor & Francis Group

LONDON AND NEW YORK

First published 2006 in the USA and Canada
by Routledge
270 Madison Ave, New York, NY 10016

Simultaneously published in the UK
by Routledge
2 Park Square, Milton Park, Abingdon, Oxon, OX14 4RN

Routledge is an imprint of the Taylor & Francis Group, *an informa business*

Typeset in Joanna by Taylor & Francis Books
Printed and bound in Great Britain by TJ Internation Ltd, Padstow, Cornwall

British Library Cataloguing in Publication Data
A catalogue record for this book is available from the British Library

Library of Congress Cataloging in Publication Data
Keller, Alexandra, 1967-
    James Cameron / Alexandra Keller.
        p. cm. — (Routledge film guidebooks)
    Includes bibliographical references and index.
    ISBN 0-415-28851-7 (hardback : alk. paper) — ISBN 0-415-28852-5 (pbk. :
    alk. paper) 1. Cameron, James, 1954 — Criticism and interpretation. I. Title.
    II. Series.
    PN1998.3.C352K45 2006
    791.43023'3092—dc22
    [B]
    2006017736

ISBN10: 0-415-28851-7 (hbk)
ISBN10: 0-415-28852-5 (pbk)

ISBN13: 978-0-415-28851-4 (hbk)
ISBN13: 978-0-415-28852-1 (pbk)

For Frazer

CONTENTS

FIGURES

1

INTRODUCTION

James Cameron: Blockbuster Auteur, Spectacularizer of Apocalypse

Every time I make a movie, everybody says it's the most expensive film in the film industry.

James Cameron[1]

You Can't Scare Me ... I Work for James Cameron

Crew T-shirt worn on *The Terminator* set

In 1998 Canadian Atom Egoyan was nominated for an Academy Award for best director for his work on *The Sweet Hereafter* (1997). He lost out to another Canadian who made a film that, as Egoyan ironically observed, was similar to his own in this: "both *The Sweet Hereafter* and *Titanic* have big crashes with ice and water that take place halfway through the film" (in Lacey, "Tale" A2). *Titanic*'s winning director was, of course, James Cameron. And whereas Egoyan's nomination for best director confirmed Hollywood's inclination at least to acknowledge art films, Cameron's win confirmed Hollywood's inclination to honor, when possible, spectacular epics that do very well at the box office, and no film has ever done as well as *Titanic*. But in so awarding Cameron, it also gave him an artistic credibility that he had theretofore lacked, though to be sure he had long been acknowledged as a master, even genius, technician. The Oscar allowed for the possibility that Cameron's work in cinema was qualitatively on a par with other auteurs, directors whose *oeuvre* was consistently both recognizable (the authorial "signature" of an auteur) and excellent (the ability of the person in charge of an industrially created product to raise it to the level of art, and himself to the level of artist).

To talk about James Cameron as an auteur is to acknowledge how very far film culture has come from the original usage of that term. To talk about *Titanic* as a blockbuster is to speak about how the film has profoundly changed what that category means. To talk simultaneously about auteurism and the blockbuster is to implicate them with each other, which is to suggest that as the notion of the auteur has become broader, the idea of the blockbuster has become discernible as something like a genre, and certainly as a format with familiar protocols. To talk about auteurism and the blockbuster together is to speak of a hybridization of categories only conceivable under postmodern conditions. For it is under postmodernism that the concepts of auteur and genre have indeed mutated far from their original intentions and understandings (originality itself being highly suspect under many postmodern rubrics).

Cameron himself certainly subscribes to a variant of auteurism: "The director is always God,"[2] he said in 1994, the year his *True Lies* became the first film with a $100 million budget. But the designation auteur is best used in a looser way with Cameron, at least on the face of it. In the traditional sense, as initiated in the 1950s by André Bazin *et al.* at *Cahiers du Cinéma*, subsequently debated in the 1960s in the United States by Andrew Sarris and Pauline Kael, and revised in the 1970s by Peter Wollen and others, Cameron is only provisionally an artist with a unique vision, and one whose entrance into either Sarris's famed 'Pantheon' (Howard Hawks, John Ford) or even his close but no cigar 'Far Side of Paradise' (Douglas Sirk) would be questionable.[3] This is not at all to say that Cameron is a hack director without a vision or a signature. Rather, it is to suggest that whereas John Ford had a more workmanlike approach in which the word artist never appeared ("My name's John Ford. I make westerns," he once famously said), and where Sirk deliberately subverted the conventions of melodrama to critique them, Cameron is neither generally subversive and working against the system in which he works, nor is he without pretenses to the idea of art in his films. If the original idea of an auteur was bound up in a strangely retrograde and romantic notion of genius, Cameron nevertheless fits that retrograde bill in his innovative nature. He has a true genius for special effects, technological ingenuity, and an extraordinary knack for giving the spectator a remarkably physical, visceral viewing experience. On one hand, Cameron is responsible for some of the most groundbreaking techniques and indelible images in contemporary cinema. When *Titanic* (1997) called for underwater camera movement impossible with existing equipment, he simply invented what he needed (as he had done before with *The Abyss*, resulting in five patents), and there is no doubt that the sight of the Terminator (Arnold Schwarzenegger) removing his own eye has become iconic in the contemporary film canon, signifying far beyond the narrative of the film itself and describing in a single image the reflexivity of vision and subjectivity in the late twentieth century.

On the other hand, Cameron is often legitimately seen as an egomaniac with far too much money at his disposal, and his films can be not just expensive but offensive. *True Lies* (1994), in which Schwarzenegger plays an American secret agent single-handedly battling hordes of generic, hysterical Arab terrorists, affronted many critics and audiences like few films since *Birth of a Nation* (1915), but with little of the sustaining film historical interest that D.W. Griffith's film offers. (In some ways it may be worse – in 1994 film culture might have been expected to have a significantly shorter fuse concerning racism than in 1915, and, re-viewed under post-9/11 conditions, the racial politics Cameron takes for granted seem symptomatic of how the U.S. became the object of such violent anger in the first place.) His technological achievements and visual and thematic consistency notwithstanding, James Cameron remains one of Hollywood's most important directors for two interrelated reasons. First, he is responsible for many of the most expensive films ever made, as well as the highest grossing film in history, *Titanic*, a film that also tied the record for most Academy Awards won.[4] Second, though Canadian by birth, he may be the most symptomatic director of American mainstream cinema of the last 20 years. As Marc Shapiro, author of an unauthorized Cameron biography put it: "James Cameron, once he steps behind the camera, has proven himself the voice of the man on the street."[5] That is, Cameron's films, with all of their technological virtues and ideological limitations, tell us much not only about what U.S. culture has to say, but also about what it does not know it has to say.

Prior to *Titanic*, it was possible to say that Cameron's genres were science fiction and action (or some combination of the two), but his most recent fiction feature, currently holding the world box office record[6] of nearly $1.85 billion in gross receipts, appears to be a radical departure, though it has always been unfair to box any of his films into one genre – they are usually hybrids of at least two, and usually a few. Still, *Titanic*'s generic difference from its predecessors makes auteur criticism a useful framework for discussing Cameron as a director. As a set of organizing principles, it helps address how *Titanic*, a film that seems generically anomalous in the largely sci-fi and action-oriented works of the Cameron *oeuvre*, is actually very much in the Cameron groove. If we can speak of Cameron's directorial signature, it comprises two major ideas. First, Cameron is obsessed with vision itself, and in ways that far exceed the preoccupation with vision any film director has. Every film he has ever made has spent a significant amount of its time, aesthetic, and narrative energy conveying to the viewer not only the requisite thrills and emotional and visceral intensity of Hollywood blockbuster entertainment, but also complex and quite serious meditations on what it means to see, both from his side as a filmmaker and from the spectator's side as a filmgoer – as well as what it means to see under broader postmodern conditions. (See Chapter 3 for a full account of this visual paradigm.)

Additionally, and increasingly, Cameron's groove has been money itself. Just as John Ford made his mark in the Western, and Alfred

Hitchcock spoke through the thriller, so Cameron, once called the Cecil B. DeMille of his generation,[7] seems to have gravitated toward the block-buster as his format, and in so doing he has helped re-define radically what that means. Significantly, he has continually pushed the limits on budgets: *Titanic*, dubbed Cameron's $200 million art film by Fox CEO Bill Mechanic,[8] required the funding of two studios, Fox and Paramount, and clinched the proposition that the more money spent on a film, the more it was likely to make – a precedent set by Cameron three times before with *The Abyss* (1989), *Terminator 2: Judgment Day* (1991), and *True Lies*.[9] Atypical of most blockbuster films in that it was neither science fiction nor, strictly speaking, action, *Titanic*, both the most expensive (until Peter Jackson's *King Kong*, 2005) and the most profitable film of all time, has nevertheless become something of a Golden Mean for blockbuster cinema. In this sense, one may legitimately argue that whatever other themes Cameron concerns himself with from film to film, one of his favorite subjects is the transparent cinematic representation of capital, and, by implication, his access to and control over it. That his films so often take a populist tone suggests that Cameron's access is not purely a solipsistic one – he seems to see himself as standing as a proxy for the millions who don't have this access, and their position as spectators is a way of participating in that access. What differentiates this circuit of exchange from a more typical director making large films for a large audience is something that becomes clearest in *Titanic*, as I shall discuss below.

In this, among other things, Cameron is a decidedly post-studio director. In other ways he more typifies the patterns of the Classical Hollywood studio system. His favorite film is *The Wizard of Oz* (1939), an exemplar of the latter, but the film that sparked his desire to make movies was Stanley Kubrick's *2001: A Space Odyssey* (1969), an exemplar of the former, which he saw 10 times on its release. This is a note-worthy event in part because *2001* was so different from the science fiction that came before it, and significantly altered the way subsequent science fictions films would be designed and made.[10]

Cameron was born in Canada and raised in an Ontario suburb of Niagara Falls. Frequent trips to the Royal Ontario Museum in Toronto,

FIGURE 1.1 Cameron's science fiction film *The Abyss* clearly shows the influence of Kubrick's *2001: A Space Odyssey*.
20th Century Fox / The Kobal collection

where he sketched antiquities, helped him become a skilled illustrator.[11] At 17, his family relocated to Orange County, California, where Cameron, after false starts in college majoring in both physics and

English literature, became a truck driver. In 1979 he went to work for B-movie king Roger Corman, who also fostered the early careers of Martin Scorsese, Francis Ford Coppola, Ron Howard and Jonathan Demme, among others, and here Cameron first began to hone his special effects techniques. Officially, his first directorial effort was *Piranha II – The Spawning* (1982), but Cameron was fired from the project after 12 days, though his name was kept on the film. Cameron himself considers *The Terminator* (1984) his directorial debut.

Called "the most important and influential film of the 80s,"[12] *The Terminator* set crucial precedents in Cameron's career. It was the beginning of the director–star collaboration between Cameron and bodybuilder turned actor turned Republican Governor of California Arnold Schwarzenegger, which has so far yielded four films (*The Terminator, T2, Terminator 2 3-D: Battle Across Time* (1996), and *True Lies*).[13] (Cameron has producer credit on *T3: Rise of the Machines* (2003), but he neither wrote nor directed it.) It was also the first time Cameron had complete control over a film from story idea to script to production deal to locations to storyboarding to special effects to editing, and this was a control he seldom if ever has relinquished. *The Terminator* also marks the start of Cameron's fascination with vision, violence, technology, strong women, money, and the nexus of representation and history. He is hardly the first director to address these ideas, but the particular nature of his engagement is altogether symptomatic of his – and this – historical moment: postmodernism.

There are two dominant traditions vis-à-vis the term postmodernism, one critical of it and one cautiously optimistic of its potentials. Postmodernism can be looked at as a problematic development in the history of politics, society and culture or as a potentially positive set of shifts, challenges and evolutions to the status quo. Where its critics (e.g. Fredric Jameson, Terry Eagleton, Jürgen Habermas, Hal Foster) see an epistemology marked by a breakdown of tastes and standards, its proponents (e.g. Craig Owens, Linda Hutcheon, Charles Russell, Robert Venturi) see an expansion or de-emphasis of, and a challenge to, those very same things.[14] Looked at with a dark eye, postmodernism has led to the breakdown and fragmentation of the subject beyond repair. It (and its adjunct poststructuralism) marks a devalorization of genius and of the author – of the very fact or possibility of authorship. And perhaps most seriously, postmodern conditions are often cited as reasons society fails to invest in progress and history. Looked at progressively, postmodernism's ostensibly fragmented subject (whose unification was likely always illusory anyway) is capable of far greater social and political radicality than ever before, and certain characteristic practices of postmodernism subvert the control of any dominant ideology which might lead to the formation of oppressive cultural canons, and can make possible a more diverse and democratic approach to historical discourse, in which power is not a precondition of the right to historicize – historicization standing in for the more obviously quotidian rights of civic engagement and civil rights.

And just as Cameron is a symptomatically postmodern director, any one of his films lends itself easily (some more than others) to readings both progressive and conservative. For example, Cameron seems at once suspicious of both Big Government and Big Business. In film after film he takes a dim view of the power of government and the inevitability of Big Business to screw things up. In *The Terminator* and *T2* government and corporations get into bed together, and the result is nuclear war and a race of genocidal cyborgs. In *The Abyss*, the Navy and a multi-national oil company are revealed as morally bankrupt by the extra-terrestrials living under the ocean floor. In *True Lies*, Schwarzenegger's government operative actually has to disobey orders to get the job done. And in *Titanic*, it's clear that a hubristic, corporate-driven desire to bring the ship across the Atlantic in record time leads directly to the disaster.

Seen as a group of films, these simultaneously progressive and reactionary readings are less likely.[15] The more of Cameron's films one sees, the more his conservative ideology comes to the fore, ironically in his apparent attachment to strong women characters set in genres like science fiction and action that are traditionally pitched to men. *Titanic* may be exceptional in Cameron's work for a fan base mainly consisting in teenage girls eager for all the Leonardo DiCaprio they can get, but this does not mean that his films, masculinist though they may be at a generic level, have not actively invited female spectators.[16]

Given when Cameron began to make these action films with female heroes, this invitation is all the more unusual. The 1980s, as Susan Jeffords has astutely argued, were the era of the cinematic Hardbody, male action heroes serially embodied by stars like Bruce Willis (*Die Hard*, 1988, and its two sequels), Mel Gibson (*Lethal Weapon*, 1987, and its three sequels), Sylvester Stallone (*First Blood*, 1982, and the two other *Rambo* sequels), and, of course, Schwarzenegger.[17] Central to the characters each played: John McLane, Martin Riggs, John Rambo and the Terminators, respectively, was the ability to achieve heroic action (killing the bad guy, or guys and restoring The Order of Things, i.e., capitalism and patriarchy) while themselves withstanding significant physical duress, damage, injury, and sometimes torture. The suffering was itself a proportionate measure of heroism.[18] Generically predisposed suffering and sacrifice as a measure of narrative centrality had heretofore largely been the province of the female protagonist of the woman's melodrama, though the suffering is not always physical, and certainly nowhere near as spectacularized. In several of his films, Cameron seems to bring these two conditions together in the lone figure of the female action hero.

If Cameron indeed has other consistencies in his films, one of the most important remains his heroic, and very often physically powerful, female protagonists. If *The Terminator*'s Sarah Connor (Linda Hamilton) is the first of these heroines, she is latent until T2, at which point her extremely muscular body competes with Schwarzenegger's for the spectator's attention and admiration. In between, Cameron made *Aliens* (1986 – the full blush of the Reagan years), which turned Sigourney Weaver's Ellen Ripley from Ridley Scott's more measured, stately and almost intellectual force in *Alien* (1979) into a reluctant but fierce Mama Warrior, who happens to have a degree from the Yale Drama School.[19]

The catalyst for Ripley in Cameron's episode of the franchise is motherhood. Given the barebones plot of *Alien*, Cameron was able to give Ripley any backstory he chose, and what he chose to fill in her decades in hypersleep between the first and second films was that she had a daughter whom the unforeseen events of the first film effectively forced her to "abandon," and when she returns to earth, she finds her daughter has died an old woman.[20] Thus is put into play her first level of maternal guilt. Told that the alien she escaped in the first film might still be roaming LV-426, the planetary outpost where the crew in *Alien* ran into so much trouble, Ripley is absolutely uninterested in going there until she's told there are families living there. "Families," she gasps, and agrees to go. Nevertheless, she remains disconnected from the violent action of the Marine Company she accompanies until they discover the outpost's only survivor, a little girl named Newt. It's at this point that Ripley begins to act like her Hardbody male counterparts, using firearms and opting for violence as something other than a last resort. The showdown is precisely the action film climax for which Cameron is known – Ripley, still human, but encased in so much technology she is almost a Terminator-like cyborg, does battle with the Alien Queen, to protect the makeshift family that has congealed in the course of the narrative. Just as the Alien Queen is about to stick it to Newt, Ripley growls, "Get away from her you bitch," and tosses the creature into deep space.

Two things are of particular interest here. First, Ripley says a "bad" word for the first time. "Bitch," so gender specific, not only signals the magnitude of Ripley's rage, but its nature as well. This points up sharply what the film has worked very hard to hide, but ultimately cannot: the Alien Queen, previously seen below ground pumping out alien eggs, is also a mother, and this final battle is between a good mother and a bad one. Not only that, but the battle is arguably (and symptomatically rather than intentionally) set in racial terms, as the white, blonde Newt is defended by her new white mother against a black predator.[21] Second, the Alien mother defeated, Newt runs to Ripley, shouting "Mommy!", which is not something we have heard her call Ripley before. Here one sees that Ripley's exclamation of "families" early on was prophetic and wishful. In the end, the family unit has been reconstructed, complete with android nanny (Lance Henrikson's Bishop), and the proposal is offered that the acceptable rationale for violence in women is in defense of their children.

Even Cameron's heroines not in the Hardbody mold have strength more typical of action heroes. In *The Abyss*, Lindsey (Mary Elizabeth Mastrantonio) seems almost to enjoy being relentlessly called a bitch – what, in Cameron's world, a woman apparently has to be to design, build, manage and save a colossal oilrig. (Indeed, where in *Aliens* the invective is uttered once and to vituperative effect, in *The Abyss* it takes on the contours of a compliment in its incessant repetition. Compliment or insult, Lindsey internalizes it by the end of the film.) In *True Lies*, even Harry Tasker's (Arnold Schwarzenegger's) once naïve wife, Helen Tasker (Jamie Lee Curtis), is man enough to throw punches not only at the enemy (male and female) once she knows the score, but also at her husband, for lying to her so condescendingly all these years.

Still, Lindsey/Mastrantonio remains a bitch, softening only when her estranged husband, Bud (Ed Harris), finally hails her as "wife" from 20,000 leagues under the sea. Helen/Curtis is just as likely to be seen as manly when she strikes, rather than as the gun-toting, helicopter-hopping fury of a woman she becomes (that is, unless she's battling Tia Carrere's villainess, at which point the spectator is treated to a precisely choreographed cat fight). Ripley/Weaver's major motivation to heroic action is almost exclusively maternal, and she can only dispense with the Alien Queen when the showdown is framed in mother vs. mother terms.

Clearly, though, the most pronounced example of Cameron's female Hardbody is the second coming of Linda Hamilton in *Terminator 2*. In the sequel to the much lower-budget original, Cameron makes two major changes: the Terminator is now the good guy, and Sarah Connor's body has made a chrysalis-like transformation, and now more resembles that of the Terminator. On the one hand this is a breathtaking spectacle: Linda Hamilton's body is as precisely cut and as beautifully ripped as Schwarzenegger's, and Cameron (who eventually married Hamilton in 1997) shoots the formal properties of her physique no less articulately (see Chapter 3). Yet that newly buffed body, which is as capable of both action and suffering as Schwarzenegger, et al., must pay for it. T2's full title, *Terminator 2: Judgment Day*, explicitly refers to nuclear Armageddon (see below). But the judgment of Sarah Connor in this film never ceases. T2 sees Hamilton's Connor, for all her action hero ingenuity, as an inferior mother to her son — Schwarzenegger's Terminator is a better mother *and* a better father. Indeed, Connor's physique exists as it does entirely to protect her son, yet the film tacitly disapproves of this kind of physical self-absorption in women, seeing a narcissism in it that it does not see in the Terminator's body maintenance. This self-care is rather seen as an impediment to the very same protective and defensive motherhood it is designed to enable. In the course of the narrative, Schwarzenegger's good Terminator pauses time and again to instruct or act as object lesson to Connor about how to be a good mother — including showing her how to sacrifice herself for her son by sending himself to his own doom in the film's climax. She refers to the Terminator as the perfect father, misunderstanding for the moment that he has the same maternal skills the film insists she lacks. Whether one reads Sarah Connor as having learned how to be a mother from the Terminator, or, more in the mold of the maternal melodrama, to have come to desire her own repression in the patriarchal system, the reeducation process that subtends the narrative seems to succeed.[22] At a crucial moment she has a gun to someone's head and finds that, in front of her son, she can't pull the trigger — her reinscription as someone with humane instincts is understood to be equal to her resurrection as a mother.

(The female action heroes of *Aliens* in the Reagan eighties and *Terminator 2* on the threshold of the Clinton years remind us of Cameron's symptomatic nature. Ripley could only act aggressively to defend the traditional family unit against the overproducing single mother of the Alien Queen. T2 reflects a more proto-Clintonian willingness to engage, however problematically and stickily, in a more polymorphous understanding of the social function of gender.[23] If

Reagan dodged the equal pay issue, and would not even say the word AIDS until very late in his term, Clinton presented a more complex relation to gender and sexuality by signing, as his first executive order, the "Don't Ask, Don't Tell" policy on gays in the military, and by earning his reputation as the serial buttocks-fondling feminist, whose particular taste in women, their excesses quite culturally feminine (curves, make-up, hair), ran aesthetically far both from his own wife and from the stars of Cameron's films. T2 resonates with Clinton-era conditions not least in this: Schwarzenegger's Terminator is, for a time, father and mother, and the new and improved T-1000 (Robert Patrick), who is made of a metal alloy that can change shape and mimic anything it touches, does not hesitate to take the form of a woman.[24] This is a long way from Schwarzenegger's predatory Terminator in the first film merely mimicking the voice of Sarah Connor's room-mate, whom he has just killed, over the phone. If neither machine has actual sexual desire, Cameron nevertheless reasserts his preference for hetero-masculine heroes by posing Schwarzenegger's muscular, unchanging bulk against the T-1000's litheness and ability to "experiment" with any organic form he chooses.[25])

Cameron's fierce women, then, tend to be pressed back into the service of patriarchy, pleasantly reaffirming the way things are in a manner equally palatable to both women and men. Time after time, Cameron has his heroines use their spunk and force to maintain the status quo. In Titanic, Kate Winslet's high-spirited, enlightened, Freud-quoting heiress, Rose, initially seems to lack the physical force of Cameron's previous heroines (though she has an exemplary turn-of-the-century feminist social stance[26]), but as the ship goes down, she seems as unstoppable as the Terminator in her efforts to free her lover from his watery prison below decks. She is as independent, willful, smart, sexy and idiosyncratically beautiful[27] as Cameron's previous leading women. And yet again, Rose, a powerful but pleasing figure of the feminine, ultimately serves both patriarchy and the owning classes she appears to spurn in favor of Jack and all that he represents. Cameron's films have a kind of bait-and-switch when it comes to their heroines, and ultimately many of his narratives provide the viewer with the Classical Hollywood closure of the union of the heterosexual couple, as well as the (re)constitution of the nuclear family, though often with a dystopic twist.

In *The Terminator*, love-struck Kyle Reese (Michael Biehn) succeeds in his mission of impregnating Sarah Connor before he is killed. In *The Abyss*, Bud and Lindsey are reunited in a finale that seems specifically to be an aquatic response to both *Close Encounters of the Third Kind* and E.T. *The Extra-Terrestrial*, seeking to erase the heartbreak of separation of the latter film.[28] In *Titanic*, Rose and Jack find true love, consummate it, and Jack (like Kyle) sacrifices his life for hers.[29] In *Terminator 2*, Sarah and John Connor and the T-101 (Schwarzenegger) briefly comprise the happy family unit, and again the sacrificial figure is the father rather than the mother. In *Aliens*, the makeshift family of Ripley, Hicks (Michael Biehn, again) and Newt (Carrie Henn) survives, though Hicks has sustained critical injuries to assure that.[30] And in the ultimate happy ending, Schwarzenegger having rescued his daughter from a skyscraper in a military jet, *True Lies*'s Helen and Harry Tasker have their happily-ever-after kiss in front of an atomic mushroom cloud.

In a film where, Cameron claims, almost everything was supposed to be received tongue in cheek ("And you know what? I'm not a p.c., candy-assed director," he once quipped[31]), this mushroom-cloud kiss reflects his fascination with the failure or betrayal of state-of-the-art technology, and yet, using state-of-the-art technology – often of his own invention – he neither questions nor problematizes it, or his use of it, to bring this fascination forward. There is good technology and bad technology in Cameron films, and this is distinct from the good and bad people who wield it. (The Terminator is an interesting example of both technology run amok and its (ab)user wrapped into one, though no one is ever in doubt that he has a maker outside of himself. This maker will, in T2 turn out, slightly circuitously, to be a black man, bringing on a whole new set of complexities.[32]) Moreover, while much is made of his frequent use of firearms and his high body counts, the technology that appears to fascinate Cameron most is not the technology of death, but the technology of representation.

The extent to which Cameron frequently sees representation as more real than the real is the extent to which he often refers (somewhat obliquely) to history and politics as accessories rather than central ideological discourses. Image in Cameron's films is more real – or more revealing – than reality. This, of course, is a sleight of hand symptomatic of a TV-era director, three of whose films have been serials (The Terminator, T2, Aliens).[33] If image says more about reality than reality, then Cameron has it both ways – his meta-images supersede the reality of the films, and yet it is clear that the film as a whole is itself a chain of images that supersedes the reality of the film audience. This particularly postmodern relationship of representation and real is seen in each of his films in a remarkably consistent way.

Among the many other important tropes of a Cameron film, perhaps the most crucial is the notion of prosthetic vision, and its implications. Cameron has yet to make a film without prosthetic vision. Titanic is no exception, and here, where it is least obvious, it is perhaps most important. For in Titanic, Cameron's use of prosthetic vision manifests what Robert Burgoyne and Alison Landsburg call "prosthetic memory" which "describe[s] the way mass cultural technologies of memory enable individuals to experience, as if they were memories, events through which they themselves did not live."[34] The implications of Titanic's prosthetic memory may be less dire than Burgoyne's exemplar, Forrest Gump, simply because the event itself does not have the import of "the sixties." But the note it strikes is no less deceptive, and may be even more so since it is part of a larger aesthetic tradition presented under the sign of Cameron.[35]

In The Terminator we are presented early on with the now famous red field of Schwarzenegger's cyborg vision. All visual information is mediated, and text breaks the world down into data – animal, vegetable, mineral, terminal. It is a method of negotiating the world visually that is distinctly non-human, distinctly technological. In Aliens, Ripley sees a great deal of the initial Marine incursion on a number of video screens, which transmit what each soldier sees (as well as the vitals signs of each – *Terminator* redux), as she sits safely inside a protective vehicle. Cameron often specifically aligns her view with that of Corporal Hicks's camera, a character with whom she will later form something of a couple. In *The Abyss*, in a direct precursor to *Titanic*, there are little video camera rovers that swim through the depths of the ocean, moving ahead of divers, a pair of scouting eyes through which Lindsey and Bud see both the oceanscape and, at times, each other. In *Terminator 2*, the cybervision is back, but in addition there is also a lengthy scene in which we observe Sarah Connor undergo some decidedly sadistic psychiatric testing. Our vision is often mediated by a video screen, which highlights the clinical power and detachment of her doctor, but also shows us a pathos the doctor can't see. In addition to all the high-tech night-sights befitting a secret agent's mission in *True Lies* – mediated vision again – the T2 video probe repeats itself as Schwarzenegger anonymously verbally tortures his own wife, who sits behind a two-way mirror. The audience often sees her through a video feed and the glass simultaneously, as well as on a television screen that abstracts her image to highlight heat-emitting areas – predictably, tears. (See Chapter 3 for detailed analyses of all of these scenes.) We can go further and include *Strange Days*, the script he wrote and produced for then-wife Kathryn Bigelow.[36] The film's foundational premise revolves around the ability to "jack in," or plug other people's visual and sensory experiences, which have been stored on disc, directly into one's own brain, a kind of hyped-up virtual reality complete with snuff films. In all of these films, this prosthetic vision simultaneously, and often paradoxically, both further distances the spectator by adding another layer of vision to the experience of watching a film, and brings the spectator closer, by reminding us through this now-conventional coding that we are, in fact, engaged in the act of watching a movie.

This thematic of mediated vision reappears in *Titanic* as Brock Lovett (Bill Paxton), captain of the present-day dive crew, cynically delivers a dramatic, made-for-the-Discovery-channel narrative to accompany the roving camera's investigations into the ship. But prosthetic vision in

Titanic is not just the technological, it is the historiographic as well. The visual-aid technologies embodied by the underwater Mir exploration crafts that lead the crew (remaining safe and dry inside their submersible) to the safe in which lies the drawing of young Rose,[37] not only moves the crew (and the spectator) between viewing paradigms, but also between two eras (See Chapter 3). And this, too, is utterly typical of Cameron.

Why and how? For one thing, with the exception of *Aliens*, these films all take place in the present, however much they move back and forth to past and future, and *Titanic* is no exception.[38] Cameron, whatever else he is, is not a modernist, nor even merely a postmodernist. He is *presentist*, and this is especially evident in *Titanic*, his single period piece, his one and only foray into history and the past. As *New Yorker* critic Anthony Lane pointed out in his review of *Titanic*, the film about a sinking ship was actually more like the two *Terminator* films than it was a "fresh departure" from them, because in all three Cameron is

FIGURE 1.2 Whether his films are set in the past or future, Cameron is a particularly presentist director.
The Kobal collection

"obsessed by the bending and shaping of time."[39] And this obsession with time becomes, in the case of *Titanic*, an obsession with history.

Cameron's obsession with history in *Titanic* brings us back to the status of both the film and its director as instantiating precisely those attributes of postmodern cultural production that critics of postmodernism like Jameson and Habermas worry about. As historian Patricia Nelson Limerick has suggested: "Each age writes the history of the past anew with reference to the conditions uppermost in its own time."[40] What can mark postmodern historicism, including that performed under the sign of cinema, is a consciousness of these conditions as factors in the shape of discourse. If every age before this one wrote in reference to its own circumstances, it did not necessarily do so with such an externalized and performative understanding of the intimate relation between *what* the history was, *for whom* the history was produced, and *whom* it served to produce it in that particular way. I certainly do not wish to suggest that historical discourse and historiography have never before had any element of self-consciousness at all – Herodotus and Thucydides are nothing if not aware of their own status as historians, as different as the implications of that term might have been at the time, and anyone who calls herself a historian will likewise have a reflexive sense of her own enterprise. Simply in debating the conditions of postmodernism, and by agreeing that, despite disagreements on the utility of postmodernity, the modes attributable to and provoked by it, and the implications for social and cultural futures (both local and global), we acknowledge that this *episteme* differs from what preceded it. It need not be hyperbolically claimed that postmodernism and postmodern forms of historical discourse are marked by a break from modernist modes, or pre-modernist modes, or any modes at all. Rather, certain traits, tendencies, models, paradigms, and methods which may long have existed, are simply becoming dominant or prevalent *in proportion* and *in relation* to other traits, tendencies, and so on. It is dangerous to claim uniqueness, even (especially) in the context of the "nothing-new-under-the-sun" mood that is one of the markers of this turn of the century. Postmodern historiography, then, is distinct from, but continuous with, previous historical modes. It is distinct not so much in its difference, but in how it achieves its ends through its means in a context that has shifted markedly since the end of World War II, and, in a more accelerated way, since 1968.

But in Cameron's case, I want to suggest, it is not so much a question of a heightened consciousness in telling history, or a revisionist desire to critique it. Rather, it is an apparent desire to *own* history, which Cameron wants to re-invest with that capital "H". In so doing, he is far more like the odious Cal Hockley (Billy Zane), whose desire to own Rose not only made him a capitalist pig, but also reduced her to an allegorical figure (not altogether progressive or feminist in the context of the film), and far less like his hero Jack Dawson, whom he has been so reviled for quoting during one of his many Oscar-acceptance speeches.[41] In making ownership claims on history, his desire to be "king of the world" is not about identifying with his young, beautiful, and doomed working-class artiste, nor even the object of Jack's affections. It is about commodifying history and selling it *qua* commodity to a public eager to buy it. This should not suggest, however, that audiences mindlessly cottoned to *Titanic* like so much Jonestown Kool Aid. Rather, it seems perfectly plausible that the film's popularity stems in part from audience identification with Cameron himself, and a desire by some of the viewing public to own history as well – and this returns us to the possibility that Cameron manifests a very industrially symptomatic corporate populism.

The nature of the history that the public who is also the *Titanic* audience aspires to own is deeply contingent. On the one hand, as Vivian Sobchak notes, there is a sustained rhetoric of "it really happened" at the base of so much fan sentiment.[42] Spectators do indeed invest in the realness of *Titanic* in equal parts, it seems, because the film gives the impression of depicting things the way they really were and because the film depicts events that really happened. But the key word here is "investment." Audiences, like Cameron, are looking for a payout, and if, within limits, Cameron plays fast and loose with the truth, it matters little to the audience as long as there is a *rhetoric* of historical accuracy attached to the film. In an extensive interview with screenwriter Randall Frakes, who had novelized Cameron's *Terminator* films, Cameron vacillates between claiming certain events are presented exactly as witnesses say they were and comfortably admitting that he changed certain things to offer a more emotional and entertaining film. Certain accounts don't wash for the director because the historical agents narrating them (e.g., Titanic's second officer, the crew member looking for icebergs who missed one) have clear motivations to lie (future employment, pressure by the corporate bigwigs, large sums of money paid by newspapers). This suspicion is par for the course for an historian, and as in any historical endeavor, doubt here functions as a vital part of rigorous research.

Elsewhere, however, Cameron reconstructs events surrounding the band playing on the deck of the sinking ship, events that determine whose account he believes about what the last song played might have been. Was it "Autumn" or "Nearer My God to Thee"? Cameron puts all of the evidence together like a responsible historian, concludes the evidence for "Nearer My God to Thee" is more convincing, but in the end concedes not only that it may not have been the last song, but, more important, "It gets complicated because there are 3 versions! And then you have to guess which version [the bandleader] would have chosen, based on his background. But that's not the version I used. I used the one I liked. The one I thought was most evocative."[43] Seeking details that will help him package his historical epic most effectively seems the only grounds for departing from historical accuracy – from throwing it overboard – which is already contingent in this instance, because Cameron is choosing from conflicting eyewitness accounts. The commodification of history wins out over history itself. Stickier still, *Titanic* suggests that the commodification of history now *is* history. Cameron's assessment of the evidence for what the musicians played brings him to this: "It became a myth that they played ["Nearer My God to Thee"] probably because it was true."[44] Even if myths can be distortions of truth, Cameron's statement seems to suggest something far closer to equivalence.

These conditions are a partial indication of how blockbusters and the people who make them are some of the staunchest signifiers of the complexity of postmodern popular cultural production. Where high and low art barriers are broken down, the relation between capital and culture can become simultaneously transparent and altogether invisible. Both happen in *Titanic*. Blockbuster films, or "event movies," such as *Titanic*, are no different from the rest of blockbuster culture in this: these cultural "events" take the place of historical events. They aspire to become history not by doing anything, but by appearing, or passing, as history. And in this they are exemplary postmodern simulacra. The claim to be the event comes before the event itself, and, thus designated, becomes the event (in attendance, ticket sales, expense, profit, merchandise, consumer ethos). It does not become history, as it pretends; it replaces history. One of the great ironies of *Titanic* and its extraordinary global popularity is that the actual sinking of this ship today would probably be a smaller blip on the historical radar screen than the film about it has been.

This obsession with history brings us back to Cameron's symptomatic nature: the assertions, both visual and thematic, that Cameron makes in his films carry with them their own repudiation or counter-criticism. His heroines are stronger than his heroes, but their strength is used to uphold patriarchy. His cinematic assertion that facts are facts is undermined by his repeated use of images that supersede what they represent. And in what may be his most interesting contradiction as a director, his films constantly criticize government and especially big business, and yet this latter is precisely what James Cameron is and does.

Titanic, the most successful film ever produced, offers up these Cameronian contradictions writ exceptionally large, and writ in an altogether contemporary font. Indeed, *Titanic*, as well as Cameron's larger project, manifests the more negative view of postmodern practice, in which spectacle replaces history, consumption takes the place of political action, and the signature merely appears to represent a signer. The visceral experience of watching *Titanic* does not move spectators to review historically the early twentieth century, or their own present, but rather to review the film. *Titanic*'s progressive claims about class do not incite its spectators to pay more attention to the plight of contemporary Jack Dawsons, but rather to consume as commodity (and therefore ultimately dispose of) the social message of *Titanic*, such as it is. And Cameron's aspirations to the status of auteur, his successful bid to be "king of the world," articulate themselves less in terms of art and entertainment than those of power itself. All of this – history, capital, and subjectivity – come under the sway of *Titanic*, but that film is only the most accomplished of a longer chain of narratives with similar effects. *Titanic*, as the world's most successful blockbuster, so expertly reframed its proposed concerns of romance, class, gender equality, technical prowess and historical accuracy as sheer commodity that it became as ubiquitous and as all-encompassing as global capitalism itself. It presents its viewers with extremely pressing and vital issues in an ostensibly rigorous historical context. But by tacitly framing its concerns in terms of consumption, it offers its audience the easy way out, while still leaving them with the impression that they have participated in something of vital importance. This spectacular aspect of *Titanic* is essential to understanding the film's popularity. "It is the sun which never sets over the empire of modern passivity. It covers the entire surface of the world and bathes endlessly in its own glory."[45] Guy Debord was defining the spectacle in those lines, but he might just as well have been speaking of *Titanic*, its maker, and its format, the blockbuster.

The *American Heritage Dictionary* defines a blockbuster as "Something, such as a film or book, that sustains widespread popularity and achieves enormous sales." This, surely, is a rather modest definition for the *Titanic* phenomenon, though it certainly fits. It also fits – far more snugly – a growing number of movies and cultural events. Thomas Schatz proposes that blockbuster films are "those multi-purpose entertainment machines that breed music videos and soundtrack albums, TV series and videocassettes, video games and theme park rides, novelizations and comic books."[46] In a general context, this is, of course, an excellent description of the way blockbusters of any medium ultimately bleed far beyond their original form into many corners of everyday life. But it does not describe the *Titanic* phenomenon very well. *Titanic* is considerably less of an "entertainment machine" than most blockbuster movies – what theme park ride could possibly come out of this film that would be tasteful enough to get off the drawing board?[47] And in some sense this makes it an exception that proves the rule, though its success has also produced other rules. It's instructive to look at the numbers, both national (that is, U.S. and Hollywood centered) and global. The following are recent figures for the top ten moneymaking films in both categories:

USA

1.	*Titanic* (1997)	$600,788,188
2.	*Star Wars* (1977)	$460,998,007
3.	*Shrek 2* (2004)	$436,721,703
4.	*E.T. The Extra-Terrestrial* (1982)	$435,110,554
5.	*Star Wars: The Phantom Menace* (1999)	$431,088,297
6.	*Spider-Man* (2002)	$403,706,375
7.	*Star Wars: Revenge of the Sith* (2005)	$380,262,555
8.	*Lord of the Rings: The Return of the King* (2003)	$377,027,325
9.	*Spider-Man 2* (2004)	$373,524,485
10.	*The Passion of the Christ* (2004)	$370,274,604

Non-USA

1.	*Titanic* (1997)	$1,234,600,000
2.	*The Lord of the Rings: The Return of the King* (2003)	$752,200,000
3.	*Harry Potter and the Sorcerer's Stone* (2001)	$651,100,000
4.	*Harry Potter and the Chamber of Secrets* (2002)	$604,400,000
5.	*Harry Potter and the Goblet of Fire* (2005)	$600,000,000
6.	*The Lord of the Rings: The Two Towers* (2002)	$581,200,000
7.	*Jurassic Park* (1993)	$563,000,000
8.	*The Lord of the Rings: The Fellowship of the Ring* (2001)	$546,900,000
9.	*Harry Potter and the Prisoner of Azkaban* (2004)	$540,100,000
10.	*Finding Nemo* (2003)	$525,300,000

International (Combined)

1.	*Titanic* (1997)	$1,835,400,000
2.	*Lord of the Rings the Return of the King* (2003)	$1,129,027,325
3.	*Harry Potter and the Sorcerer's Stone* (2001)	$974,557,891
4.	*Star Wars: The Phantom Menace* (1999)	$925,600,000
5.	*Lord of the Rings: The Two Towers* (2002)	$924,291.552
6.	*Jurassic Park* (1993)	$920,100,000
7.	*Shrek 2* (2004)	$916,421,703
8.	*Harry Potter and the Goblet of Fire* (2005)	$891,994,357
9.	*Harry Potter and the Chamber of Secrets* (2002)	$878,987,880
10.	*Lord of the Rings: The Fellowship of the Ring* (2001)	$867,683,093[48]

Eight years ago, when Titanic was just sliding out of theatres, the lists looked like this:

USA

1.	*Titanic* (1997)	$588m
2.	*Star Wars* (1977)	$461m
3.	*E.T. The Extra-Terrestrial* (1982)	$400m
4.	*Jurassic Park* (1993)	$357m
5.	*Forrest Gump* (1994)	$330m
6.	*The Lion King* (1994)	$313m
7.	*Return of the Jedi* (1983)	$309m
8.	*Independence Day* (1996)	$305m
9.	*The Empire Strikes Back* (1980)	$290m
10.	*Home Alone* (1991)	$286m

International

1.	*Titanic* (1997)	$1.15bn
2.	*Jurassic Park* (1993)	$563m
3.	*Independence Day* (1996)	$505m
4.	*The Lion King* (1994)	$454m
5.	*Jurassic Park: The Lost World* (1997)	$385m
6.	*Forrest Gump* (1994)	$350m

7. *Men in Black* (1997)	$336m
8. *Star Wars* (1977)	$319m
9. *Terminator 2: Judgment Day* (1991)	$312m
10. *E.T. The Extra-Terrestrial* (1982)	$305m[49]

The comparison is instructive, for it tells us almost at a glance the profound effect that Titanic has had on blockbuster culture. In the older list, though there is a slight tilt to the most recent calendar year (Titanic, Men in Black, Jurassic Park), there is a far more even distribution of release dates (1970s, 1980s, 1990s) than in the most recent chart. There, Titanic is number one in revenues, but it's one of the older films on both lists. Most of the films in both the U.S. and international top ten have been released within the last several years.

Calculated purely by the numbers, films crop up further down the the 1997–98 list that we might not expect, like the Dustin Hoffman cross-dressing comedy Tootsie (1982). Even GoodWill Hunting (1997) and The Full Monty (1997) seem strange sharing the spotlight with dinosaurs and both star and sinking ships.[50] On the newer list, only Home Alone and The Sixth Sense seem to have made it there by word of mouth. This suggests two important things about the traditional assumptions girding the definition of blockbusters. There is a stereotypical blockbuster, and even Forrest Gump, the Oscar-winning, homily-mumbling, cross-country running, shrimping village idiot savant with the box of chocolates does not fit into it. We generally expect blockbusters to be experientially onomatopoetic, which is to say we expect them to bust our blocks. We tend to expect them to be loud and noisy, and to have impact that is visceral first, emotional second, and intellectual a sometimes distant third. Largely we think of action films, science fiction, and adventure films – exactly what Cameron does – when we think of blockbusters. Or rather, when the studios lay out that much money, they are unlikely to do it on quiet films, even if the profit potential is almost as great. So at some level, blockbusters have both a broad generic definition, as well as an aesthetic and generic attitude. However true that was when Titanic was still in theaters, it is all the more so today.

Indeed, that more accurate implication of the word blockbuster – something so popular that there are lines around the block to see it – is almost an impossibility these days. Since the release of Titanic, more and more films open on so many screens that there are virtually no lines and no waiting. This practice has also resulted in the expectation that any film with blockbuster expectations make its money in the first week – precipitous drop-offs in box office receipts from the opening week to the next are now routine, so that a huge opening weekend no longer guarantees sustained profits. Significantly, then, Titanic is nowhere to be found in the list of top 20 grossing weekends, nor even top grossing single days. However, starting with its fourth weekend, it holds the record for highest grosses for a film in its fourth through 18th week. Filling out the rest of the top 25 spots is My Big Fat Greek Wedding (2002 – see below).

There is, then, a big difference between films that make loads of money, and films that are blockbusters, and some of that has to do with reaching the audience at a certain volume. Were it simply a question of cost to profit ratios, it would be fair to say that The Full Monty and Four Weddings and a Funeral (1994) were also blockbusters, since, not only do they both hover around the $200 million mark in ticket sales (which seems to be the new magic number in the U.S.; $250 million is the new global figure), but their profits also far exceeded what they cost to make. By this logic, Cameron's original Terminator might modestly fit the bill, having made $37 million on a budget of only $6.4 million. But this is hardly the full picture: as massive as the profit margins are for these inexpensive films, there is no Four Weddings and a Funeral culture, no Full Monty ethos. Titanic, more than any film since Star Wars or Raiders of the Lost Ark (1981), has both. Moreover, unlike Indiana Jones or the many Star Wars films, Titanic stands alone, with no real possibility of a sequel. This may, in fact, have something to do with its popularity. Knowing that, the spectator had better get it now if she's going to get it at all. Insofar as a sequel almost always requires at least a memorial, or mental re-viewing of the film that preceded it, it might be suggested that Titanic's repeated viewings by many spectators is in some small part a replacement for the sequel that can never be.

Of course, there is obviously more to the blockbuster dynamic, and increasingly the issue isn't just the magnitude of profit but the magnitude of outlay as well. It's not hard to see the impact Titanic has had on subsequent big-budget Hollywood filmmaking. It seems to have given permission for guiltless outsized bottom lines. (The new Hollywood studio dictum: "Ya gotta spend money to make money!" Not necessarily different from the old Hollywood studio dictum.) Inflation alone simply cannot account for the fact that of the 20 most expensive films ever made, only one (Waterworld, Kevin Costner and Kevin Reynolds, 1995) was made before Titanic.[51] Some blockbusters, to be sure, are quieter than others, and the buster part of that neologism seems hardly to apply. These films are more like blockburrowers. For example, The Full Monty, Good Will Hunting and My Big Fat Greek Wedding, made their money quietly and/or slowly, relying as much on word of mouth as advertising (as did Four Weddings). Not so with Titanic.

With Titanic there could be no word of mouth, no quiet building of support for a cinematic gem discovered by a lucky few who became disciples spreading the news. The film had no secret, and was unknown to no one. Nearly everything about Titanic seemed to be pre-spoken. The success of The Full Monty in the U.S. had much to do with "I just saw the most charming British film last night." Good Will Hunting thrived on "and you know those two cuties, Ben and Matt, actually wrote it too!" Nia Vardalos's My Big Fat Greek Wedding was a story whose Cinderella qualities existed as much in her own life as in the film, as was well documented. Titanic's word of mouth was bold headlines in the mainstream press that picked up steam right about when the film missed its original release date of July 2, 1997. And even when the copy spoke favorably of the film's quality, the slug lines and ribbons predominantly whispered doom. In its August 1997 issue, Premiere magazine ran a story called "Cameron's Way," which was announced on the journal's cover with a ribbon screaming "Titanic Panic! What's Really Going Down."[52]

The article was one of many that spoke of Cameron's meticulous devotion to detail, his relentless pursuit of the perfect reconstruction of the ship, using the original blueprints. In *Premiere*'s December issue, the month *Titanic* was released, the extensive feature was titled "Magnificent Obsession," and the slug line read, "the closer he gets to the brink of disaster, the nearer director James Cameron gets to filmmaking genius. Dispatches from the set of 'Titanic.'"[53] The notion of an entertainment reporter filing a dispatch gave the project the quality of a war, possibly even a quagmire. Nevertheless, in that article, more pre-spoken word was put forth: about the $3 million that Fox Studios had given the director so he could dive down to the actual Titanic *twelve times*; about the technology, such as a crush-proof camera, that Cameron invented just for the shoot; about the 90 percent of scale replica of the Titanic constructed in the world's largest water tank (also constructed for the shoot, about which more later); about the PCP in the chowder. Lest anyone think that Cameron were a no-sacrifices free-spender, he also repeated the information that he had given back his salary, or, as he put it, "I'm doing it for free."[54]

When, months later, it became clear the film would likely crack the billion-dollar mark, *Premiere*'s rhetoric shifted from nay-saying to boosting. It ran a story called "Cameron Is God," which less than subtly suggested that Cameron, having given up his back-end deal, should now be rewarded with a sizable bonus for turning the world's most expensive film into the world's most profitable.[55] (In the end, Cameron was well compensated. The director suggested that this was because of the intricacies of agreements made during the shoot: "Now they owe me an enormous amount of money . . . Let that be a lesson to us all. They stepped over a bar of gold bullion to pick up a penny."[56]) Likewise, *Entertainment Weekly* Monday morning quarterbacked *Titanic*'s success, seeking to learn lessons for next time from a *sui generis* event.[57] So radically has *Titanic* altered the expectations for and contours of the blockbuster that, though profits were actually up industry-wide from the previous summer, it was nevertheless considered an unspectacular year, since no film had cracked the $200 million mark. As *Entertainment Weekly* began its article on the subject:

> It will go down in history as the summer the blockbuster turned lack-luster. Halfway to Labor Day, something strange is happening in entertainment: This year's putative event movies are taking their sweet time cracking the $150 million mark, and it looks increasingly unlikely that *any* of the films will see $200 million … Even the most sun-struck event-movie devotees are detecting the scent of block-buster breakdown in the air.[58]

To toll the death-knell of the blockbuster was not only unwise, it was also unoriginal, and is less true in the wake of *Titanic* than it has ever been. The pertinent point is that, next to *Titanic*, these high-grossing films suddenly appeared less successful, and that seemed momentarily to affect audience perceptions of them. Two full seasons later, audiences were still "imprinted" with *Titanic*, and the largeness of the typical blockbuster could not distract them. Or as *Entertainment Weekly* put it, audiences were suffering from "chronic post-blockbuster fatigue syndrome."[59] They certainly seem to have recovered. On the most recent global box-office list, only *Jurassic Park* was released before *Titanic*, and seven of the top ten films have been released since 2001.

Other than marketing, perhaps the clearest indication of *Titanic's* influence is the presence of other later action and adventure films on the list that seem to have internalized the template of the "human element" or emotional register of *Titanic's* narrative. Films like Peter Jackson's *The Lord of the Rings* trilogy may be as loaded with special effects and set-piece action sequences as *Titanic* was, but, still seeking the Holy Grail of marketing, they are no less invested in foregrounding the intense personal relationships between Sam (Sean Astin) and Frodo (Elijah Wood), Aragorn (Viggo Mortensen) and Arwen (Liv Tyler), both of which are heavily romantic, and romanticized, just like Jack and Rose. Likewise, *Spider-Man* also emphasizes the love story between Peter Parker/Spider-Man (Tobey Maguire) and Mary Jane Watson (Kirsten Dunst).

Most recently, Jackson's King Kong invested in a love triangle among man, woman and ape. King Kong was the film that at last broke Titanic's budget record (to the dismay of Universal Pictures, the studio that released it), but logged a "mere" $50.1 million in domestic (U.S.) box-office receipts after its first weekend, falling $25 million below predictions. While some saw this as cause for alarm, many did not, and Universal executives pointed to King Kong's similarities to Titanic: its cost overruns, its three-hour-plus running time, its widespread critical acclaim and good consumer word of mouth, its less than spectacular first weekend, all of which suggested Jackson's film might enjoy the same longevity as Cameron's.[60] That, like Jackson's successful Lord of the Rings trilogy, King Kong seemed to have taken on board Titanic's more personalized ethos seemed clear. As Entertainment Weekly film critic Lisa Schwartzbaum wrote of King Kong's ability to be both stunning spectacle and heartwarming woman–simian love affair:

> Indeed, reliving these pleasures puts me in mind of Titanic, however imbalanced the weight of fantasy fiction versus that of historical fact might seem to be. In both pictures, the old world gives way to the new under duress (the ship and its prewar class system sinks, the untamed animal is defeated atop the swanky Empire State Building). And in both, the rush of pure, movie-going satisfaction is precious.[61]

Titanic makes clear that by the end of the twentieth century the block-buster film had developed a two-part definition. Obviously, any film that makes enough money, especially one that does it quickly and dramatically enough, is regarded as a blockbuster, and this quality is only amplified by a film's potential market tie-ins (e.g., Star Wars, Batman, The Matrix, Spider-Man), which extend public consciousness of and desire for the film into other aspects of life, from fast food to sunglasses, soundtracks to special edition Jeeps, Halloween costumes to cell phones, beer to bed sheets. But it is only with the release, press and success of Titanic that the other side of the definition becomes absolutely clear – as does the fact that this aspect of blockbusters is relatively new (suggesting that blockbusters are indeed mutating into something as distinct as a genre). A film can be a blockbuster before it is even released, and even if it doesn't make any money, if enough time, money and industrial and popular attention are invested in it and focused on it. Even before it was released, *Titanic* was, in that sense, already the biggest blockbuster of all time.

Because they have developed this two-part description, blockbusters need to be looked at not only in terms of success but also in terms of failure. For every Hollywood boom there is a bust. The boom: *Finding Nemo*. The bust: *The Adventures of Pluto Nash* (2002). The boom: *The Ten Commandments* (1956). The bust: *Cleopatra* (1963). The boom: *Star Wars*. The bust: *Heaven's Gate* (1980). This last boom and bust couplet has particular relevance to *Titanic*. The generation of blockbusters out of which *Titanic* might be said to mutate is obviously that of *Star Wars*, but the parent nobody talks about is *Heaven's Gate*. There's a tendency when doing thumbnail histories of the film industry to think in terms of what worked, looking at failures as cautionary tales of what not to do again, and regarding successes as the keys to formulas that, *mutatis mutandis*, can repeat themselves. But this positive focus (and I am overstating the case somewhat) gives us an incomplete picture. Blockbusters that fail can be just as influential in their voice-from-beyond-the-grave way. *Heaven's Gate*, after all, is, at least mythically, the film that sunk the Western for all time – or at least for the duration of the Reagan–Bush years. And while *Titanic* is in many ways discernible as a descendant of the *Ten Commandments/Godfather/Star Wars* line, it is just as much the successful offspring of Michael Cimino's epic failure. Cameron's now-legendary attention to detail, his insistence that everything from the carpets to the lifeboat davits come from the same manufacturer as the real Titanic, his certainty that, even though no one on or off the screen would ever see them, the luggage tags had to be authentic down to the handwriting, has its heritage in Cimino's similar maneuvers for *Heaven's Gate*. He seemed in some ways to want to surpass Cimino's obsessive limits. "James Cameron wanted everything exactly as it was on the real *Titanic*," said Rolando Navarro, operations manager at Foxploration, the movie theme park that grew out of the huge studio built in Rosarito, Mexico to shoot the water scenes.

"Even the china was authentic, and Cameron had it go down with the ship, just like it did in real life."[62] Moreover, Cameron's insistence on a period piece, a romantic epic (a genre so contrary to his area of proven expertise), as well as his insistence that the audience would give him all the time he wanted,[63] smacked of Cimino's insistence on spending his *Deer Hunter* Oscar clout to make a Western – the one genre that in the 1970s appeared to be undeniably on its way out.[64]

But that is where the films part ways. *Heaven's Gate* was too political and too leftist-populist to appeal to a film culture which, worn down not only from the Vietnam War but from the protest culture that developed to oppose it, was turning towards a cinema that was either more entertaining, more solipsistic, or both. *Titanic* is, at the end of the day, utterly apolitical, or, at any rate, differently political from its own very overt claims, which resemble those of *Heaven's Gate* itself. *Heaven's Gate* anchored its politics firmly in the conventions of the Western genre (even if those conventions were, by that point, as much those of the counter-Western), using those very conventions to effect a critique of the dominant ideology. *Titanic*, emerging as it did under the conditions of full-blown, even late-stage postmodernism,[65] also frames its epic story in the generic framework of the historical romance. The difference is the enthusiastic nostalgia of *Titanic*'s generic attachment – nostalgia symptomatic of a strong and significant current in postmodern cultural production. The ease with which *Titanic* presented history, via nostalgia, as an eminently consumable commodity, goes a long way to explaining its popularity. Oddly enough, it is this aspect of *Titanic* which may have had the most profound effect on another blockbuster that seems to be its opposite in many ways: *The Matrix*, in spite of its philosophical ruminations and diatribes against the numbing effects of consumer society, presents a future that has a nostalgia for the past that resembles our present (even as it suggests that our present is the imaginary future of *The Matrix* – dizzy yet?), and offers up its cautionary tale as an eminently consumable product.

Because *Titanic* presents class dilemmas in commodified form, they must also be palatable enough to consume. But the unromanticized representational conventions of working-class life are dreary indeed, and Cameron ultimately wants none of them, though, as with other types of conventions in the rest of his films, this is just what he appears to desire at first glance. The capaciousness of Rose's beautiful first-class stateroom is ironized by her fiancé's efforts to imprison her in it. Escaping to the cramped lower decks, Rose finds true joy as she kicks up her heels, in spite of the lack of space. Indeed, the romantic implication in *Titanic* is that the working class is happiest when it can crowd together, and that the human density poses no challenge to the almost genetic will the poor have to dance no matter where, no matter what, when they hear a fiddle or an accordion (this chillingly implies that the poor also have an almost genetic will to poverty, which seems borne out insofar as Jack doesn't survive long enough to refute it). So, in the end, Rose the adventuress has led a life both like Jack's, and like the one he wanted her to lead. But it is the rich version of that life. By leaving us with the image of an anonymous post-rescue Rose, which we connect to the bohemian image of a much older Rose at the potter's wheel, Cameron urges us to believe that Rose has really renounced her class. But she hasn't rejected it at all, only the most obviously repugnant values. These values: boorishness, materialism, a tendency to treat people (especially women) like objects, are no less extant in the non-filthy rich, though you'd never guess from Cameron's depiction of the folks in steerage. As the pictures she has brought to her stateroom on the present-day ship narrate – Rose the Hollywood starlet, Rose the Jane Bowles-esque desert explorer, Rose the Amelia Earhart-avoiding-the-Bermuda-Triangle-style aviatrix – Rose has led an adventurous *but expensive* life. Paralleling the Picassos, Degas and Monets she brought into her stateroom earlier in the film, these are pictures of a life that, relative to Jack's, is only slightly less privileged than the one she gave up.

It is at the end of this idiosyncratic, but nevertheless lush life, that Rose throws away the Heart of the Ocean. Intended to be the ultimate renunciation of materialism, throwing away the necklace is also readable as a slap in the face to Jack's memory. And this too, oddly enough, is an

FIGURE 1.3 Rose wearing the Heart of the Ocean as she is sketched by Jack.
20th Century Fox / Paramount / The Kobal collection

aspect of the film's popularity.[66] No doubt the necklace is contraband, the insurance company would be on her in a minute, and legal hijinks would ensue. But in her final impish gesture, she is not acting like Rose, or even like Jack. She is acting like Cameron. Rose's ultimately wasteful gesture of throwing away the diamond (and luxury is nothing if not about waste) may be very expensive ideologically, but the audience won't be out more than ten bucks for it. Given how much Cameron has spent on the film (a fact which virtually every audience member would have known), and given that the final act of narrative closure is one in which Rose performs an act of waste which is only ever the prerogative of the very, very rich, the audience is, for a very small fee, made momentary shareholders in this upper-class ethos, while still being allowed the moral high ground of those in steerage.

In his biography, *Dreaming Aloud*, James Cameron remarked, "Some people say less is more. No. More is more and too much is never enough." I have spent the bulk of my attention here describing the ways in which the film that best instantiates this tenet, *Titanic*, is actually more like Cameron's other films than it is a move away from them, as well as how that film has reset the terms for subsequent blockbuster films and blockbuster culture in general. So it is worth returning to what, precisely, marks those previous films. Two words seem best to describe the interests and tone of all of the films he's made: spectacle and apocalypse. Almost every Cameron film is rife with spectacular chases, fights, shoot-outs, explosions, rescues, and other action staple set pieces. But what distinguishes these spectacles from those of other action and science fiction directors is that they are invariably wedded to an apocalyptic vision or consequence. In the *Terminator* series, nuclear war is the overarching threat, and Sarah Connor's post-traumatic stress disorder-like nightmares are all about a world-ending nuclear blast. In *True Lies*, the nuclear is a romantic punch line, but when combined with the comical expression of anxiety about the nuclear family that is the other narrative thrust of the film, it amounts to a kind of humorous rumination of what's to be lost if one kind of nuclear is detonated on the other. In *Aliens*, Ripley, newly maternalized, has no problem with nuking the alien-riddled planet to smithereens after her escape vehicle has left its orbit – again suggesting the link between the nuclear family and nuclear anxiety.[67] And in the pre-nuclear, pre-World War era world of *Titanic*, the sinking of the ship seems as apocalyptic as anything else that was on horrible offer in 1912. But, resituated in a post-9/11 United States, what is of interest is the realization that Cameron has not made one of his apocalyptic spectaculars – or almost anything else – in the almost ten years since the release of *Titanic*. Indeed, since *Titanic*, he hasn't directed a narrative fiction feature film at all.[68]

In one way, though, Cameron almost doesn't have to. One extraordinary circumstance that speaks to his symptomatic nature is the extent to which, post-9/11 and in the quagmire of the allegedly accomplished mission of the Second Gulf War, some of his films can be read in ways almost opposite to what one might have on their original release. Take *Aliens*, which I have argued ultimately glorifies the military and the traditional family structure at the expense of an arguably feminist hero (as one might have seen Ripley more easily in *Alien*). Looked at in the context of the current U.S.-led invasions of Afghanistan and Iraq, it is much easier to see the drama of the soldiers as (clearly marked) working-class, often non-white individuals being used by a military structure that no longer defends vaunted democratic values, but instead colludes with private enterprise (The Company can easily be seen as an equivalent to Halliburton), and who are up against insurgents (the aliens) who wouldn't even be on that planet if the humans (all U.S. citizens) hadn't invaded it first. Likewise, *Titanic* can be re-read after the fall of the towers in a way that connects the two tragedies. Though one was an avoidable accident and the other a terrorist plot, in both cases the magnitude of the casualties produces a desire to comprehend the events one person at a time. In movie terms that means offering up just a few individuals to represent the thousands for whom audiences have neither time nor head space to work through. Looking at *Titanic*'s Jack and Rose, only one of whom got out alive, or the old couple in steerage who lie down in bed, close their eyes, smile because they are together and wait for icy doom, or the mothers looking for lost children in flooding hallways, can now bring to mind any number of heartbreaking final cell phone calls, messages left on answering machines, workers who told their colleagues to go on without them, colleagues who refused to, heroic first responders, and so on. Seeing the brutishness of Rose's fiancé and the arrogance of the ship's designer might now bring to mind a different White House than was in power when the film was released. This was obviously not Cameron's intent, but the release in 2005 of a special collector's edition of *Titanic* will be purchased and screened by audiences whose history may be profoundly inflected by the events and aftermath of 9/11, and their re-interpretation of the film may reflect that.

These about-face readings suggest the suppleness with which Cameron's films move through U.S. culture and history. Crowd-pleasers though they are, they are certainly not, with the possible exception of *Titanic*, films for all people (children as spectators are more or less prohibited from a Cameron audience by rating, if not in actual practice). Nevertheless, the sum total of Cameron's work does, as

I have suggested, produce a very specific if flexible range of populist positions.

Indeed, the sum total of Cameron's work exceeds works he has actually made, and the contours and magnitude of Cameron's influence on blockbuster culture at times manifests in bizarre ways. In season two of the successful HBO drama "Entourage," Cameron played himself directing the fictitious rising young film star Vincent Chase (Adrian Grenier) in a fictitious film version of *Aquaman*. In the opening episode of season three of "Entourage," Chase learns that *Aquaman* has captured the most successful opening box office figures of all time. In the summer of 2006, *Pirates of the Caribbean: Dead Man's Chest* opened to record box office numbers ($132 million in its first three days). On 10 July 2006, cable news network CNBC's anchorman Joe Kernan reported that *Pirates* beat out "the previous three-day record *Aquaman* at 120 [million] plus, which just beat out the 115 million which was set by *Spider-Man* back in May of 2002." Merely by playing himself on an HBO series that was entirely about the lives of fictional young Hollywood players, Cameron was, however briefly, presumed to hold a *Titanic*-scale record for a film he had not made – and likely never would make.[69]

Martin Scorsese's *Gangs of New York* (2002) concludes with a final shot of the southern tip of Manhattan, the World Trade Center still standing, a monument to its loss, as well as to the understanding that the romance of the immigrant narrative the film depicts is significantly responsible for the towers coming to exist at all. Spike Lee's *The 25th Hour* (2002) explicitly takes place in the aftermath of the 9/11 disaster, and where Scorsese calls the towers momentarily back into being, Lee offers up an extended shot from the luxurious high-rise apartment of an investment banker that looks down over the eerie nocturnal work at Ground Zero.[70] Cameron is certainly not the only significant director who has yet directly to address 9/11 in some way – and he most probably never will.[71] But that Cameron hasn't might mean something slightly different. If, as I have suggested, representation is more real for Cameron than the real, and that this representation that supersedes reality also takes the place of actual historical reckoning by offering pseudo-history as a consumable product, then in 9/11 Cameron's filmic visions have taken on an unexpected corporeality. For the tragedy of 9/11 was not only a trauma of unprecedented magnitude and nature in recent U.S. history. It was, via the inevitable media attention, the repeated viewings of horrific and theretofore-unimaginable images, the narrativization of sacrifice and heroism, rendered both spectacular and spectacle. And the responsive rhetoric of the George W. Bush administration – particularly from the Chief Executive himself – was twofold: "smoke 'em out of their holes," as he famously remarked of the terrorists (wanting Osama bin Laden "dead or alive," Wild West style), and "go shopping," as he exhorted American citizens, as a way to prove that Al Qaeda had not scared them. Laced throughout all of this was the nuclear specter of North Korea, with Iran and Iraq part of Bush's Axis of Evil. So the spectacle of 9/11 resulted in an apocalyptic mindset (which in Afghanistan and Iraq were rapidly made real for the overwhelmingly non-terrorist populace) at the level of foreign policy coupled with a complementary consumerist mindset at the level of domestic policy. So the United States currently finds itself in a strangely Cameronian everyday world: spectacle, apocalypse, and consumption have all become inextricably linked. If Cameron, like most mainstream directors, aims to make films that offer two hours of an altered reality, he may find it more difficult now that reality has caught up with Cameron.

Portions of this introduction have previously appeared as "James Cameron," 50 *Key Contemporary Filmmakers*, Yvonne Tasker, ed. (London: Routledge Press, 2002) and "'Size Does Matter': James Cameron as Blockbuster Auteur," in *Titanic: Anatomy of a Blockbuster*, Gaylyn Studlar and Kevin Sandler, eds. (New Brunswick, NJ: Rutgers University Press, 1999).

2

GENDER, GENRE, TECHNOLOGY AND CLASS:

Key Debates about the Work of James Cameron

Compared to classical Hollywood directors like Alfred Hitchcock or global contemporaries like Wong Kar-Wai and Atom Egoyan, James Cameron initially received relatively little academic treatment. This is in part because Cameron's enormous popularity was at first discernible only in relation to the films, and not the man who directed and wrote or co-wrote them. That is, people went to see *The Terminator*, but they did not go to see a James Cameron film. This is not simply because it was his first major feature film – Spike Lee's first film, *She's Gotta Have It* (1986), after all, was as much about the rise of a new young director, one who was awarded the *prix de la jeunesse* for his debut at Cannes, as it was about the film itself. Even *Aliens* was a film that audiences went to see as much because it was a sequel as because it was made by the director of *The Terminator*. But it is also in part because Film and Media Studies tend to call on shifting objects as their methodologies shift, as the works discussed below show. All of this has certainly changed with the release of *Titanic*, a film that occasioned the publication of an entire volume of scholarly work on the film and related events. Critical debate in non-academic contexts has been more sustained. While plenty of it is very shallow (i.e., thumbs up or thumbs down), much of it is extremely thoughtful, and it is often not productive to separate it from articles that appear in scholarly journals or books.

It comes as no surprise that the critical debates about and analyses of the work of James Cameron have to do with two main things: 1) deciphering the socially significant subtext of films whose generic nature suggests that they are "just entertainment," and, not unrelated, 2) illuminating the particular way that competing ideological discourses reveal and resolve themselves (or fail to) in these films. As I began to suggest in my introduction, some particularly rich areas of academic consideration have to do with gender, genre, class and ideology. Though there are a number of works that examine trends and tendencies over a span of Cameron's films, the majority of the critical discourse on Cameron's films tends to look at one film at a time – say, *The Terminator* in the context of science fiction, *Aliens* in relation to the rest of the *Alien* series, or *Titanic* in the context of consumer or blockbuster culture. Scholars and critics have applied almost every conceivable contemporary method of analysis to Cameron's films: psychoanalysis, feminism, cultural studies, Marxist analysis, ideology critique, political science method, and more. Given how often Cameron makes a film that becomes a cultural touchstone (especially for United States culture), it is not uncommon for the scholarship to take on an especially conversant tone, addressing previous scholarship and courting the possibility of sustained debate. In this, as with other directors to whom the auteur designation might far more easily (if no more wisely) be given, Cameron's work has proved rich ground not only for its own sake, but also for the way his films function so effectively as powerful gateways to cultural critique.

THE TERMINATOR AND THE TERMINATOR AS ACADEMIC OBJECTS

One of the earliest scholarly considerations of Cameron's work came in 1986, from Constance Penley, a feminist film scholar who, using psychoanalytically-based methodologies of film analysis, teased out the

Oedipal configurations of a film whose narrative premise of the father going back in time to produce the son who sent him back in time to do that very thing offered up a particularly interesting conundrum.[1] For Penley, *The Terminator* slotted easily into the category of dystopian science fiction films, and, as it had generated so many intertextual spin-offs, was a plainly postmodern one.[2] But it was also a critical film, one that troubled itself not with technology *per se*, but with what human beings did with it, and why, and suggested "causes, rather than merely reveal symptoms."[3] Its critical stance relied on the deployment of an aesthetic of "tech noir" (also the name of a nightclub in the film), in which Cameron made clear that the machines of today – and their users – had clear implications for the machines of tomorrow, as well as for future human subjectivity. Answering machines and those who spoke into them, Walkmans and those who listened to them, and of course, firearms and those who fire them, coalesced into a kind of vanishing point out of which appeared the Terminator himself, machine and human in combination, *cyborg*. That this technology was imbricated in a time-travel narrative was crucial for Penley, as it inevitably produced a number of paradoxes, centrally an Oedipal one. (Indeed, machines and time travel are quite distinct in *The Terminator* – there is no time machine as such.) Such time-traveling paradoxes, Penley argued, had much in common with the "time traveling" back to childhood in which the analysand engages when speaking to the analyst. In significant cases, such as Freud's Wolf-Man, this time travel brought the patient back to the Primal Scene, the fantasy of witnessing, overhearing or otherwise apprehending sex between one's parents, potentially (again in the realm of the fantastic) observing one's own conception. "The idea of returning to the past to generate an event that has already made an impact on one's identity," Penley suggests, "lies at the core of both the primal-scene fantasy and time travel."[4]

What is the *The Terminator*'s primal scene? The last words that Kyle Reese flings at the Terminator, along with a pipe bomb, are "Come on, motherfucker." But in the narrative logic of this film, it is Kyle who is the mother fucker. And within the structure of fantasy that shapes the film, John Connor is the child who orchestrates his own primal scene, one inflected by a family romance, moreover, because he is able to choose his own father, singling out Kyle from the other soldiers. That such a fantasy is also an attempted end-run around Oedipus is also obvious: John Connor can identify with his father, can even *be* his father in the scene of parental intercourse, and also conveniently dispose of him in order to go off with (in) his mother ... One could argue that *The Terminator* treads the path from fantasy back to reality precisely because it is able to generalize its vision, to offer something more than this fully, though paradoxically, resolved primal fantasy. The *generalizing* of the fantasy is carried out through *The Terminator*'s use of the topical and the everyday: as we have seen, the film's texture is woven from the technological litter of modern life. ... If *The Terminator*'s primal-scene fantasy draws the spectator into the film's paradoxical circle of cause and effect and its equally paradoxical realization of incestuous desire, its militant everydayness throws the spectator back out again, back to the technological future.[5]

These circularities and paradoxes took on uniquely generic contours. Penley even offered the idea that, in an age where gender difference meant less and less in real, everyday terms, "it is science fiction film – our hoariest and seemingly most sexless genre – that alone remains capable of supplying the configurations of sexual difference required by the classical cinema."[6] And sexual difference was articulated not in the traditional questions of male vs. female, but rather in the genre-specific questions of human vs. other. Turning briefly to Ripley in *Aliens*, a film Penley considered far less successful in challenging the norms of gender and subjectivity, she concluded, "even when there is not much sex in science fiction, there is nonetheless a great deal about sexuality, here reduced to phallic motherhood: Ripley in the robot expediter is simply the Terminator turned inside out."[7]

To be sure, there were other scholarly accounts of *The Terminator* that focused on other elements of the film. Penley treated the narrative

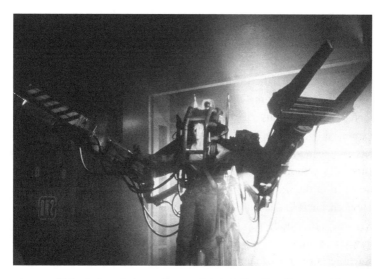

FIGURE 2.1 Ripley in the robot expediter parallels both the Alien Queen and the Terminator.
20th Century Fox / The Kobal collection

paradoxes of the film's plot in relation to her specifically psychoanalytic feminist concerns. Maintaining a feminist analytical mode, Karen Mann addressed the narrative *qua* narrative, specifically looking at the ways it enacted the narratological split between story (what happens) and discourse (how those events are presented to the spectator).[8] For Mann (and for feminist narratologists in general), an analysis of *The Terminator*'s discourse was crucial for what it revealed about the power relations both inside the story and outside of it in the industrial and social contexts of the film's production. Articulating who controls the story, produces "a measure of who or what is controlling the body and mind of the human person being implied or constructed by the story,"[9] that is, what kind of spectator the film desires to have receive it. Emphasizing the same paradoxes that Penley does, Mann suggests that *The Terminator* is unusual for the way it not only reorders discourse (not at all uncommon in film narratives – think of the multiple flashbacks in *Citizen Kane* (1941), for instance), but also disrupts conventional story time, forcing us to ask: "what is the new logic of its story time, and how pervasive is the effect of that logic on related issues of desire and subjectivity, and hence on narrativity[?]"[10] Part of Mann's provisional conclusion is that "the dilemma the narrative will try to call up and contain is created by the antithetical movements of time and desire, so that the impossibility of the solution for the dilemma of desire is expressed by the impossibility of the time scheme."[11] If the central subject of the narrative is the Terminator itself, Mann suggests that the (diegetic) author of his story is actually John Connor, an entity who is not seen in the story, though he is constantly mentioned and to whom other characters constantly refer. Like Penley, Mann notes that Connor's fantastic and wholly psychoanalytic motivation is to choose his own parents, as well as to govern his mother's erotic desires. Existentially, she notes, Connor has another vital authorial motivation: if he does not "author" his father and mother, he will never be born.

Mann goes on to articulate the levels at which Kyle Reese and Sarah Connor also author the narrative through their desires, variously for romantic sex (via a photo given to him by John, Kyle has always loved Sarah), sex for conception (John Connor's imperative to Kyle when he sends him back in time), and survival (Sarah's imperative if she is to give birth to John). Moreover, unlike many critics who attribute the authorship of the film itself only to James Cameron (a seemingly natural consequence of auteur criticism), Mann attributes it to Cameron and Gale Ann Hurd (who were co-screenwriters), implying a bi-gendered authorship outside the film that mirrors that which obtains inside it. Finally, linking time and desire, she writes:

> By tangling the time scheme … Cameron and Hurd have shifted the balance of power in this conflict. First, the film makes clear the high cost of [this Oedipal] agenda for man as father: Kyle becomes expendable at the moment his son is conceived. Next, although the narrative does play up the placing of Sarah in a position to fulfill her sexual role in a cultural plot, by privileging her contributions as a subject who *makes* the men who they are in the film, the narrative

contains or limits the significance of that moment when Kyle succeeds in making love to her. Hence the film can permit the viewer to
accede (and respond) to certain facts of our dominant sexual/cul-
tural narratives while conceiving of ways in which those narratives
might be distorted and redefined. Insofar as culture overlays biology,
it works to achieve (if not desire) consent from woman.

   The Terminator offers several ways to get woman to say "yes": by
threat of force (the Terminator); by the ideal of motherhood itself
(John Connor); and by emotional response (Kyle Reese). That culture
cannot continue without the mother is clear. That Sarah Connor
consents is equally clear. But that the story expresses doubts about
real sexual congruence in all of its dimensions, is most clear of all. If
there is a way to say yes without succumbing to history as an expression of time and culture, the authors of *The Terminator* haven't found
it yet.[12]

The Terminator, then, may have moments of explicit Oedipal attachment
and disruption. In other words, the desire to exert authority over the
Primal Scene (as Penley has it) exists, but the rationale for it (one's
very existence) may exceed specifically Oedipal desires, and the whole
scenario relies on choosing a paternal object who will be desirable to
the mother, a desire bound up in the mother's own desire to produce
the child who desires (to author) the scene (and the self) in the first
place. And this maternal desire as authority can be read as a feminist
one. That this is all provisional, for Mann, returns us to her focus on
narratology: the complexity of the shifting authorial positions makes
subjectivity and gender inside and, potentially, outside the film, unstable.

   This instability was also symptomatic of specific instabilities in U.S.
culture. Susan Jeffords's influential book *Hard Bodies: Hollywood Masculinity
in the Reagan Era* describes a shift from a more traditional model of cinematic hero in the pre-Reagan era to the "hard bodies" of the Reagan
years.[13] Whatever else constituted pre-Reagan cinematic masculinity
(most of which continued to obtain), it had not previously so explicitly been considered as opposed to a "soft body," one that could be

marked as soft in a variety of non-normative ways from gender (female) to ethnicity (non-white) to diseased, drug addicted, or otherwise implicitly immoral when held up against the straight white male normativity of the hard body. For Jeffords this hard body links the movies to the image of President Ronald Reagan (who was also known as the Hollywood President), but also crucially links Reagan and the movies to the nation's image of itself, one that appeared to have gone soft under President Jimmy Carter. Emphasizing the relations among popular culture, politics, and subjectivity more than either Penley or Mann, and implying that films may be less psychic reflections *per se* and more policy ones, less about collective unconscious and more about collective symbolism,[14] Jeffords argues that "the depiction of the indefatigable, muscular, and invincible masculine body became the linchpin of the Reagan imaginary; this hardened male form became the emblem not only for the Reagan presidency but for its ideologies and economies as well."[15]

The Terminator poses an interesting problem under this rubric, for its central character, Schwarzenegger's Terminator, is hardly the film's hero, though it far more perfectly – and literally – embodies (up until the moment of its crushing) every corporeal aspect of the hard body. (It is not so much the Terminator's villainous position that makes it anomalous as a Reagan Era Hard Body as it is the cyborg's utter lack of ideology or morality – it is *programmed* to eliminate Sarah Connor, it hasn't *chosen* to.) By comparison, the love-struck sperminator Kyle Reese is only required to be a hard body in one way, and only in one organ, and his mortal sacrifice, though heroic, is inconsistent with the rest of the era's hard body heroes (Rambo, *et alia*). But by the sequel, *Terminator 2: Judgment Day*, the Terminator has undergone significant changes, changes that, to Jeffords, are a sort of inverted repetition. This makes T2 a crucial transitional text as 1980s Reagan Hard Body masculinity shifts into its modulated (and ultimately Clintonian) form in the 1990s. Sent back in time to protect 11-year-old John Connor from the even more advanced T1000, the Terminator still has the unstoppable cyborg body, but now he is under orders (from the John Connor of the future who sent him back to protect the prepubescent John Connor of the film's present) never to kill a human being (instead he merely wounds them, seemingly in some kind of moralistic proportion to their goodness or badness). John Connor himself is neither the capable rebel leader nor the glimmer in his mother's eye of the first film, but, at last visible in the film, is a bratty juvenile delinquent who must begin to accede to his adult heroic status in the course of the narrative. (It must also be said that his appearance is fairly androgynous – as is that of the T1000, and that this is more than a function of his age, it is also a harbinger of the androgynous figure of Leonardo DiCaprio in *Titanic*.) And, most visibly, Sarah Connor is still the concerned mother, but she has been so vocally concerned about the apocalyptic future that she has been committed to a mental institution (recall that Kyle's testimony in the first film also brought about a designation of madness from the LAPD psychiatrist). And in that confined setting, she has rebuilt her body by the least technologically advanced means (pull ups, chin ups and sit ups using only her bedroom furniture), and is no longer the deer in the headlights waitress of the first film, but has herself become something akin to the Terminator's hard body.

It is this inverted transition that is of greatest interest to Jeffords. In Sarah Connor's failure to be a normative maternal figure to John, a narrative gap and a subsequent necessity open up in which she is "gently replaced"[16] by the Terminator. Here the inversion of the Terminator begins to expand. He is not only, as Sarah herself admits, an exemplary father. He is also, in effect, an exemplary mother. This, to all intents and purposes, reverses the politics of the previous *Terminator* film. Regarding films generally as symptomatic of their cultural moments (and, I would add, Cameron being a particularly symptomatic director), this comes as little surprise for Jeffords. That he is may be symptomatic of some crucial shifts in American masculinity from the ethos, ideology, and policies of Reagan to those of Bush I, who famously spoke of wanting a "kinder, gentler" nation and, implicitly, national character. Jeffords offers that supplanting the mother in T2 not only has implications for gender, it also has implications for racial identity and subjectivity, as she describes:

FIGURE 2.2 The transformed Linda Hamilton as the transformed Sarah Connor.
Carolco / The Kobal collection

The Terminator offers the ostensible explanation for why men of the 1980s are changing their behavior: they learned the old ways of violence, rationality, single-mindedness, and goal orientation (there is no one more goal oriented than the first Terminator ...) were destructive. And the solution to the dilemma? ... [F]or the hard-bodied man to learn from his past (future?) mistakes to produce a change in character, a "new," more internalized man, who thinks with his heart rather than with his head – or computer chips ... [L]ike the Terminator, [African American Skynet inventor Miles Dyson, who offers to destroy his own invention rather than let it lead to world destruction] leaves behind him not only a woman and her son, but the future of the entire human race ... [M]asculinity transcends racial difference, suggesting that the forces of change ... not only cross racial boundaries but draw men together. What more unlikely alliance than a white-skinned killing machine from the future and a dark-skinned benevolent scientist from the present? ... [T]ogether they give human life to the world. Yet, in keeping with the racial imbalances that mark Hollywood films of this period, the Terminator leads the way in this crusade, with the black scientist learning from it and following its lead ... Where humanity was the common denominator that erased racial difference in the first film, now fatherhood erases the difference between all "new" men, whether machine or human ... *Terminator 2* can offer up to these [white male] viewers not only a panacea for their feelings of disempowerment, but it can reinforce the culturally designated culprits of that scenario in the guise of technology, machines, active women, and men of color in managerial positions.[17]

In spite of its strongly leftist anti-nuclear stance, the film remains conservative at the level of racial politics.

One might easily ask how this film could be symptomatic of a presidential administration whose policies and their effects ultimately differed little from its predecessor. And one might wonder how *Terminator 2* could reflect the delicate steps needing to be taken by an administration that followed one of the most popular in U.S. history, but that also did wish to repudiate some of the preceding policy, or at least distinguish itself *as* itself. To address this, Jeffords returns to the dual ideas of repetition and inversion as essential to articulating a post-Reagan paradigm of masculinity.

> ... [T]he film manages to reveal the "new" masculinity/father, but to excuse the "old" one as well. For though the Terminator must sacrifice itself in order to prevent a destructive future, the film's plot makes it clear that ... *it is not his fault* ... The Terminator has to sacrifice itself not because it was "bad" or harmful or even useless but because others around it misused its components. Comparably, audiences can conclude that the aggressive and destructive 1980s male body ... may not have been *inherently* "bad" but only ... misunderstood, just like the Reagan policy of SDI and increased military armaments. And who *does* understand this obsolete but lovable creature? None other than John Connor, the "new" man himself.[18]

If the Bush administration and its concomitant desires for male subjectivity did not exactly throw the Reagan baby out with the bathwater, they did not publicly and warmly invite it to stay, and they learned a valuable lesson from Reagan's Teflon presidency. That intractability and immobility became as risible for Reagan as for Rambo, and, as Jeffords notes, as easily self-parodying. T2 can be seen as symptomatic of the Bush ethos precisely for its apparent ability not to negate Reagan hard body masculinity but to rewrite it in those kinder, gentler terms.

Susan Jeffords's *Hard Bodies* exhibits a general tendency in Film Studies starting in the early 1990s to move away from traditional or feminist psychoanalysis toward practices of Cultural Studies (which Film Studies itself had influenced not least simply by taking cinema seriously).[19] Seeing the intimate, if not necessarily intentional, connection between what popular audiences saw on their screens and the conditions of their social and political lives, Cultural Studies analysis takes popular culture on its own terms (which is not to say that the object of study dictates the outcome of the analysis), is wholly inter-disciplinary, and, rather than maintaining rigid distinctions between high and low, in and out, takes an inclusive rather than an exclusive view of what constitutes culture. For Sharon Willis, whether by conse-quence or necessity, this inclusion also includes a reflexive awareness of the place of the critic: she is both part of the sector of the public sphere (contemporary audiences) that comes and goes from films and other media events, and whose relations to these individual events are unstable and in the moment, and is also simultaneously removed from, other than, that sphere.[20] In terms Cultural Studies struggled with early on, the critic may be no more or less a "cultural dupe" than any other consumer.[21] Or, rather, she may be at once critic and dupe.

In her essay "Combative Femininity," Willis examines *Terminator 2* and "the conditions that produce the ambivalently thrilling and men-acing figure of the murderous female hardbody, along with the con-flicted responses that she evokes."[22] Willis generates two key ideas in this piece, one touching on general social anxieties and ambivalences about "pro-life" and "pro-choice" stances in U.S. culture in the early 1990s, the other to do with the uneasy intersection of white feminism and black male professionalism in the context of cinematic representa-tion. As Willis asks, "Why do white women's hardbodies seem to be propped on the 'ghosts' of African American men?"[23] In both matters, *T2* appears to be ideologically incoherent; that is, it is a movie that is, as Robin Wood memorably suggested of *Taxi Driver* (1976), *Looking for Mr. Goodbar* (1979), *Cruising* (1980), and other films of the 1970s, a film that does not know what it wants to say.[24]

The contours of the film on the subjects of gender and race are also something Lisa Kennedy takes up, and I shall attend to her version of that discussion in the next section, emphasizing here Willis's reading of reproductive rights as more or less somatized – a methodological holdover from psychoanalysis, by *Terminator 2*. That is, cultural anxieties about reproductive rights, justice and authority, about which the con-versation in the Reagan–Bush I 1980s was uneasy and contentious at best, eventually emerge in a displaced representational and narrative form in popular movies, nowhere more so for Willis than this one. On the subject of reproductive rights, T2 "continually interrupts the already iconic reconstitution of the nuclear family." This is bound up not only in the specifics of the film's plot, but also the exigencies of the science fiction genre in the 1990s. Indeed,

> [T]he film offers a knot of ideological lures. While it seems to trumpet the privilege of a nuclear family unit headed by some version of a heterosexual couple, producing this image within a discourse whose key word is "choice," it also radically undercuts the ideological binding together of biology, paternity, masculinity and phallic authority … In the end … the best father will wind up at best a relic, at worst a piece of junk, recycled in a vat of molten liquid … Collective anxieties about new reproductive technologies fit coherently within the science fiction frame, preoccupied as it is with technology's own "reproduction," or proliferation, and with the breakdown of distinctions between the human and the machine … T2's last scene confirms … this [as we understand the Terminator] cannot "self-terminate." So Sarah Connor must become his "terminator." Thus, specific issues of women's autonomy and rights over their bodies are subsumed into more general anxieties bearing on technology's impact on individual self-determination and the status of the body.
>
> … T2 plays on the familiar social anxieties about women's autonomy that are sharply evident in newly escalated abortion debates, but it does so in the context of other anxieties about unstable identity, about the erasure of difference, and of our ability to "tell" the difference. The film sets Sarah Connor's resemblance to the Schwarzenegger terminator against its dystopian fascination with the figure of the T1000, the "bad" terminator, a protean cyborg that can assume a variety of forms, composed as it is of "a mimetic polymer alloy" … Equally intense fantasies about women's autonomy and about the failure of difference emerge in the conjunction of the combative female body and out-of-control technologies. In this case, the technologies have come to look like the technologies of identity.[25]

For Willis, then, T2 stakes out neither a pro-abortion and women's reproductive rights stance, nor its opposite. Rather, filtered through the particularities of the science fiction genre as it circulated and was received by audiences in an early 1990s context, the film, specifically in the way its poles of "good" and "bad" kept shifting (not something one could say of The Terminator), was a telling reflection of the multitude of points where desire and anxiety met on this matter.

On the face of it, there is no particular reason, in the context of Los Angeles, that the Terminator would best blend into the city by being designed with a white skin. Arguably, Cameron, as a white man, was only exercising prerogatives of likeness and a general white centrality in representation when he wrote the character. (That general white centrality appeared also to be a market imperative – with very few exceptions, e.g., Will Smith, Wesley Snipes, a central black character could not draw a white audience.) In the first film, the Terminator, as a villain, is opposed to two white lovers, and racial politics seem less relevant. (Less relevant only inside the film's diegesis – as Amy Taubin

FIGURE 2.3 The ad hoc nuclear family in the explicitly anti-nuclear *Terminator 2*.
Carolco / The Kobal collection / Rosenthal, Zade

FIGURE 2.4 The Terminator's whiteness is, if not arbitrary, certainly contingent.
Carloco / The Kobal collection

points out, below, even when racial difference is not explicitly on the screen, it is strongly implied not only in Cameron's films, but in so many films of the Reagan Era.) But with the casting of Joe Morton as the scientist whose technology leads to the invention of the Terminator, race emerges as a major focal point. Black motorist Rodney King had been beaten by four white police officers on March 29, 1991, and, while T2 did not have these events in mind while it was being made, its release on July 3 of the same year certainly put its representation in the context of a national concern with that event and its larger implications about race relations. Questions of power, violence, and race were everywhere, and that T2, perhaps even more than its predecessor, both implicitly and explicitly troubled itself with the idea of what constituted a body, a human, a subject, and a citizen could not be read without an eye to how race played into those questions.

Lisa Kennedy, then a critic for New York's *Village Voice*, suggested that if white spectators could ignore the implications of racial representation in cinema, black spectators could not, and that this was a sustained historical truth of film-going in the United States.[26] Indeed, the black spectator is never simply an individual. Marked as Other by dominant white culture, and self-marking as a counter-strategy, she may also bring a heightened awareness of her relation to the "collective body" provisionally known as "the black community." Kennedy's account of watching T2 in a predominantly black audience marks the way that Joe Morton's scientist Miles Dyson oscillates between being an improvement over the stereotypes of Toms, coons, mulattoes, mammies and bucks that Donald Bogle so famously lists in his account of cinematic images of African Americans, and its recapitulation.[27]

> Without a doubt, the Metropolitan Cinema is ones of the best places to see an action pic. The excellent "Awwh shit ... Kill him!" call and response of an audience makes movie-going like it oughta be. But still, who couldn't be thrown by the sight of an African American scientist ... being chastised ("it's you people who have destroyed the world!") and not scream "Whoa!" ("Who, black men?!?"), and then wonder why the collective body continued to root and respond after that moment. Is there some more compelling (though perhaps unconscious) logic than the simple "that's entertainment"?[28]

Kennedy's description of the call and response emphasizes the embodied spectator, one who is not just a pair of eyes, but a sensual as well as sentient subject. These embodied spectatorial conditions, heightened by choice, Kennedy implies, in some African American reception contexts may relate directly to two intertwined concerns: the preoccupation with bodies in T2, and the general preoccupation with bodies in a number of critical postmodern discourses.

> [T]he conceit of an adult hero reprogramming a cybertool to save his boy-self (making him more his father than his own father could be) is easily the most groovy metaphor for the work of postmodern history available. This is what history is like for the collective body; it is a tool to reengineer the past, get in there, fix it up, guarantee a future.

With history conveniently declared deceased – an untimely death to say the least – even the less conspiracy-minded of us can't help feeling that it's been murdered in order to prevent us, the collective body, from resuscitating it, exhuming it, performing an autopsy, doing whatever it takes to bear witness to the atrocities and triumphs to which it's been privy. This is, of course, one of the aims not only of Afrocentrism, but of multiculturalism and feminism.

The collective body wants to know.[29]

Kennedy explicitly links the black subject to the problems of historical discourse under postmodernism. History's alleged end under postmodern conditions poses particular problems for a constituency whose status as disenfranchised and enslaved people – partial people (3/5 to be precise, as designated by Article 1, Section 2 of the U.S. Constitution (1789) and abolished by the 13th amendment in 1865) – was predicated on their erasure from history *qua* citizen. Watching a black actor embody scientific brilliance, but also be accused (by a white mother) of being responsible for the end of humanity in a film made by whites with white money for a (default) white audience inevitably incites, for Kennedy, questions about how any individual black spectator's response bears on the black community or collective body's response. That is, in responding to a cinematic representation, how is that same response itself representative – or not – of a larger cultural and historical constituency?

Was there ever a time when the collective body moved and spoke as one? Not likely. And is that ... desirable, or even possible? ... There is a tremendous push (ours) and an opportunity (let's not forget the pangs of a hungry marketplace) for more representation, more film, more images, more, more, more ... [I]f individual blacks can speak only for the collective body, then exactly how much of it is there to be carved up and sold off? ... [W]ill we become slaves to the collective body? Forced always to speak for it and to its needs? And scared to death that if we don't, we won't be allowed to say anything; or if we misrepresent it for the sake of ourselves we will be expelled, we will not exist?[30]

So, even an afternoon at a mainstream movie that is "just entertainment" evokes the powerful problems of self-representation in the face of representation by dominant culture. Kennedy illuminates that for black spectators desiring a critical stance in relation to cultural production, the problem is not only how to navigate dominant representational modes like film, but also how to navigate the (myth of the) black community. That attending an action film would touch off such a consideration is only natural. As Kennedy suggests, "It's not a surprise to find film in the midst of this growing discussion of the collective's identity. Film because it feels extraordinarily powerful – all that money and narrative and pleasure – and because historically it is how America looks at itself."[31]

Most of the scholarly attention paid to The Terminator and subsequently (and perhaps especially) to T2 tended to the gender relations among Schwarzenegger's Terminator, Michael Biehn's all too human man Kyle Reese, Linda Hamilton's radically different portrayals of Sarah Connor, and what all of these had to do with how Edward Furlong's John Connor would grow up – how the implications of the gender and subjectivity models obtaining among the three adult principals would determine what kind of man John would become, and, of course, what all of this said about current cultural, social and political conditions. All of this while still recognizing, as Penley et al. did, that the outcome in question had already been significantly determined by John Connor himself. Relatively little attention has been paid to the T1000, the antagonist of the sequel. Doran Larson contends that this machine is, in fact, at the heart of what T2 has to tell us about individual American citizens and their relation to political conditions.[32] "The Liquid Metal Man of Terminator 2 exposes ambiguities in the American body politic that have existed for over three hundred years," writes Larson. "In contrast, the reprogrammed T101 suggests a body politic as cyborg and offers false assurances of popular control over mass democracy under late capitalism."[33] For Larson the status of the Liquid Metal Man (LMM) and the T101 in T2 are not completely legible without seeing them as shifts from the status of Kyle Reese and the first incarnation of the

Terminator in the earlier film. Moreover (and correctly presuming that the majority of the audience of any sequel has in fact seen the original), how we read the newly reprogrammed T101 ("Arnold Jr." as Larson has it, echoing the general Oedipal cast of the films' narratives) inevitably asks us to re-read the T101 from the first film, the second reading largely co-opting the first, as it also corresponds to shifts in society's relation to technology – particularly technologies of violence and of self – between 1984 and 1991. Larson is careful to maintain a connection between his reading of postmodern and late capitalist conditions and longer American traditions of Christian Puritanism (which, for Larson, can roll easily into fascism) and populism:

> It is no mystery that we are witnessing the cynical populism of Hollywood: presenting Arnold Jr. as a champion of individualism set against the extension of precisely those global forces which could *afford* to create *T2*. What endears such sleight of hand to an American audience is a long-standing Yankee faith in progress and the benevolent teleology of all technical innovation. For even today, particularly in the advent of breakthroughs in medical technology (including robotic prostheses), Americans continue to want to believe that, in the words of John C. Kimball writing in 1869 (and despite four recent years of evidence of what technology could do to human flesh), "The great driving wheel of all earthly machinery is far up in the heavens, has its force and direction supplied immediately from Omnipotence."[34] Moreover, we are also offered the moralizing satisfaction of demonizing precisely that cycle of consumerism (sequelization) in which we are caught. We are allowed to feel triumphant over the global Skynet even as we watch films bounce from satellites, from the extant "earthly machinery ... far up in the heavens." This ... truly is a pleasure of late capitalism.
>
> I have noted that we identify with Arnold Jr. because, like Kyle, he is vulnerable to wear and damage ... and records this damage in his material body ... Arnold is subject to time and the existential status of his own history. [But the LMM] is himself the popular face of con-

sumerism ... [N]ow suburban housewife, now policeman, now shining cutlery, now checkered floor, now security guard, now mother, [he] represents commodities, consumers, and the security apparatus that protects private property. In one morphing gestalt, he is the mass consumer/commodity nexus and a guard against its undisciplined indulgence ...

The original T101's threat is that of the military industrial complex turning against its creators, a threat that nonetheless confirms technology's proper conception as a servant to humanity as commodity *producer*, and ultimately proves beatable by a wage-earning, time-clocked laborer, Sarah Connor. The T1000 is, instead, the faceless-ness of retail consumerism ... Its antecedents are not in production but in retail consumption.[35]

Ultimately the correspondence of the T101 and T1000 to two ideas of America's body politic results in yet another contradiction, one that for Larson is altogether postmodern, insofar as it exhibits the idea that "the historical prior is no longer the culturally fundamental."[36] Through the corporate mass media presentation that T2 is, the audience reads an apparent condemnation of that media. Yet the T1000, in its ability to morph, also rejects (in a way the T101 does not) the more traditional idea of the head of state as head of the national body politic – an idea Larson suggests has always been problematic in American democracy for the ways it seems to risk a return to the same figuration under a monarchy. But, mired in late consumer capitalism, this is at best a disingenuous representation of new democracy. Rather, the T1000 also represents John Berger's formulation that, in late capitalism, consumer choice "takes the place of significant political choice."[37]

ALIENS AND/IN THE *ALIEN* SERIES

Aliens is unique among Cameron's films in this: not the only film he has made in a series, it is the only film he has directed in a series not of his

own making. He undeniably and crucially put his own stamp on the
Aliens series – so much so that David Fincher, director of *Alien*[3], felt
obliged to obliterate the nuclear family built in Cameron's installment
by killing off Hicks and Newt at the very beginning of his film.
Nevertheless, much scholarship on *Aliens* takes the film as one of a distinct set of components whose narratives are tightly bound up in and
responsive to each other, rather than simply containing the same characters on a new mission (e.g., *Rambo*) or facing a new situation (e.g.
Lethal Weapon). (Far fewer works take the series on after *Alien Resurrection* is
released, as if to say that the cloned Ripley, in not being the genuine
article, was also not quite worthy of the same consideration.[38])

For Amy Taubin, then film critic for New York City's *Village Voice*, that
the (then) trilogy had three different directors and only Sigourney
Weaver and Lance Henriksen as consistent acting presences simply
exacerbated the extent to which each film was a touchstone for current
social anxieties. (She was not alone in this. See Thomas Doherty
below.) Taubin saw *Alien* as a response to the loosening of sexual mores
in the 1970s. After feminism and gay activism, after Stonewall in 1969
and Roe v. Wade in 1973, "the aliens didn't bother with the niceties of
sexual difference."[39] With Ripley landing on an all-male penal colony,
and the alien moving like a virus, *Alien*[3] stood clearly for Taubin (and
many others) as an AIDS allegory. But the middle installment was
something else, an affirmative mix of science fiction, action and military epic that produced an entirely different reading of the alien, who,
in this case, was neither sexual infiltrator nor fatal virus.

> A Pentagon-inspired family-values picture for the Reagan 80s, James
> Cameron's *Aliens* (1986) is the most politically conservative film of the
> series. A marine squadron does hand-to-claw combat with an alien
> army that has destroyed the inhabitants of a planetary outpost. New
> Age assault rifles and grenade launchers are fetishized, as is the
> nuclear family. "Familes," breathes Ripley in horror when she learns the
> identity of the victims … *Aliens* reestablishes sexual difference in both
> human and alien spheres. Although the dialogue implies that the aliens

are as indiscriminate as ever in their choice of hosts, on screen it's a female human who suffers the involuntary Caesarian births. Similarly, it's the alien queen who, guarded by her warriors, lays the eggs.

Like *Alien*, *Aliens* climaxes with a one-on-one between Ripley and the alien. In the second film, however, the scene is structured as a cat fight between the good mother and the bad …

However thrilling the entrance of Ripley in the power loader (she's transformed into a cyborg), the image is immediately tarnished by the obviousness of her line, "Get away from her you bitch," addressing the alien who's about to do something terrible to the cowering Newt. The misogyny of the scene has often been analyzed on a psychosexual level as the refusal of the "monstrous feminine," of the archaic, devouring mother. But it also has a historically specific, political meaning. If Ripley is the prototypical, upper-middle-class WASP, the alien queen bears a suspicious resemblance to a favorite scapegoat of the Reagan/Bush era – the black welfare mother, that parasite whose uncurbed reproductive drive reduced hard-working taxpayers to bankruptcy.[40]

In fact, the typical welfare beneficiary during the Reagan Era was more likely to be a child under the age of 18, and by the end of the Reagan–Bush years, black women accounted for only one-third of women on welfare.[41] That the nation imagined the average welfare recipient more along the lines described by Taubin has a great deal to do with how the figure was represented in popular culture, on television shows, both news (where the images were disproportionately black and female) and fiction, and at the cinema.[42] What's particularly powerful about Taubin's reading is that she makes a claim for the audience's ability to read race allegorically (not uncommon in cinema, especially science fiction). In times when a subject is "unrepresentable," this is a culture's only recourse. Take the Vietnam War, almost entirely absent from U.S. film screens during its commission (though ever-present on TV screens), but strongly implied in a whole slew of Westerns from *The Wild Bunch* (1969) to *Little Big Man* (1970) to *McCabe and Mrs. Miller* (1971).

But in this case, the ease with which an audience might read race into the Alien Queen seems in fact to have to do with how many direct images of black welfare mothers proliferated on big and small screens during the same period.

To be sure, there were other rubrics under which that same Alien Queen figure and the vaunted nuclear family structure of Ripley, Hicks, and Newt could be considered, such as their relation to a broader category of the militarization of what seemed to be the domestic sphere, as Paul Virilio did. A central concern of political and technology theorist Virilio's work is the interconnection between war and cinema. So intimately are they linked in and to post/modernity that, to him, they are major determinants of our everyday perception. As he demonstrates in his prescient book *War and Cinema: The Logistics of Perception* (1984), technologies of war and vision achieve a kind of vanishing point, such that images of war do not document war, they *are* the war. So, for example, television viewers frequently saw the first Gulf War as a series of "clean" executions of bomb drops, as seen from a video camera fixed to the bomb. For Virilio this is not disconnected from the (only apparently) more quotidian creation of "newshounds," on whom networks like CNN rely for footage such as that from the Rodney King beating. Indeed, one might extend Virilio's thinking to suggest that the aleatory quality of the motorist just passing by with his camera has superseded our awareness of how rigid and preset news outlets are in where and when they locate and position their cameras, and this rigidity is of a piece with the rigidity of Hollywood film production under multinational corporate capitalist conditions.

Some years after *War and Cinema*, Virilio turned his attention to the particular alienation produced by *Aliens*, using a specific film to outline how closely related the rhetoric of film and war could be, not least because so much military technology had made its way, unmarked as such, into civilian life:

> What we have before us is the most recent avatar of the *propaganda fiction* that has been in vogue for some time in the United States ...

[Despite being set in the future,] the film celebrates a contemporary weapons system, a more or less direct descendant of the infamous "electronic battlefield" first deployed by the U.S. Army in Vietnam, then brought home to the Mexican border (and elsewhere) for use against illegal "aliens." (The film's dialogue explicitly refers to the problems of border infiltration: a Marine says of a Hispanic woman soldier carrying a ... rifle, "Somebody said 'aliens' – she thought they said 'illegal aliens' and signed up.") ...

Why would a science fiction film place such emphasis on the realism and verisimilitude of the actors' and actresses' equipment and weaponry? The answer, in the words of the director: "*To make the spectator feel somewhat at home in the midst of the battle.*" This is why the film's design elements are calculated to facilitate identification with the fighters – which is probably one of the film's most original aspects.[43]

Cameron has done something in fact quite unusual for a science fiction film set in the future. Rather than present the spectator with technologies and attendant ideas that are plausible, though not currently possible, Cameron has offered up something quite close to current technology, giving it only the thinnest of futuristic glosses. This aids and abets the feeling of being "at home in the midst of the battle," which in turn produces particular ideological effects not unrelated to those operating in a more domestic framework in Amy Taubin's assessment of *Aliens*. Virilio describes the Loader, the masterful operation of which helps naturalize Ripley with the platoon of Marines (she may not want to fight, but she is gifted with a technology that is a vital part of support operations, and so she earns their respect), but which later serves an even more important function.

[T]he Loader at the end of *Aliens* strikes one more as raising the curtain on a new order of military technology, the pseudo-cyborg, than as the finale of the film's promulgation of familiar military hardware. On the other hand, it really only raises Ripley to a level of brute strength commensurate with the mother alien – who, in any case, gained a vestige of subjectivity, a maternal wrath, when "she" saw Ripley exterminating her young. Thus, the *family* that formed the pretext of this neocolonial intervention ... figures as the basis for conflict ... *Aliens*, despite its gallery of monstrous morphology, had to invoke the raison d'être of the militarized family, the presence of child-like innocence. For Ripley, it provided justification for the military feats of Valor: little Newt, the orphan who somehow survived the aliens' siege of her colony. She is only an alibi, though, a foil used to justify and stimulate the viewer's jubilation at the extermination of undesirables. And how could viewers react otherwise when this traumatized innocent reenters the social sphere in fits and starts – by giving a thumbs up, saluting and saying "affirmative" and so on?[44]

Virilio puts "she" in quotations marks, rendering the gender of the Alien Queen more provisional, pointing to its strategic nature, as well as the way that the cultural definition of the feminine gradually overtakes the biological definition as the film moves towards its climax. Indeed, when, in defending Newt, Ripley famously cautions the Alien Queen to "get way from her, you bitch," we can see the biological (bitch is only a technical designation for a female dog who breeds) collide with the cultural (bitch is not a nice word to call a human woman, but it's obviously not a nice word to call an Alien Queen, either). Where Taubin emphasizes the way that viewers would read race into that gender, in the form of the mythic black welfare queen, Virilio suggests that the maternal wrath that engenders the Alien Queen also stands against the nuclear (in both senses) family created by events in the film. Far from a typical, if unplanned family, this is a militarized one, and Newt's accession to the vocabulary of a soldier is simultaneous to her accession to the status of daughter (clinched by her cry of "Mommy!" to Ripley after the Alien Queen is ejected into space), which is itself necessary to form the mother/father couple of Ripley and Hicks. (They are mother and father far more than husband and wife. As Hicks says when giving a locator bracelet to Ripley, it doesn't mean they're engaged.) But for Virilio, this militarized family is merely the contemporary American family with its veil of domesticity removed.

Likewise, but more specifically cognizant of the relations between war and cinema than Virilio, Thomas Doherty reads the *Alien* trilogy symptomatically, as Taubin does, also suggesting each is reflective of its moment. But he historicizes the trilogy in the context of crucial shifts in the science fiction genre, specifically the great divide between science fiction before *2001: A Space Odyssey* (1968), and after. "Where pre-2001 science fiction was targeted at teens, low budget, technically primitive, and intellectually stunted," Doherty writes, "post-2001 science fiction was mass marketed, well financed, state of the art, and intellectually challenging, a genre of big budgets and big ideas."[45] The shift in industrial conditions was matched by a shift in narrative, from a genre that anxiously interrogated what was out there to one that uneasily questioned what was within and among us. All three installments of the trilogy also shared certain fundamental traits of postclassical Hollywood, including the breakdown of traditional boundaries between genres, and the deliberate and overt "cross-pollination" among genres.[46] Specifically, *Aliens* was a hybrid of science fiction, horror and the combat film. And it was a hybrid that audiences accepted easily not only as the result of broader postmodern conditions (hybridity being a central marker of postmodernism), but also, for Doherty, because the film's audience had been trained in the conventions of television spectatorship as much as, and simultaneous to, those of film spectatorship.

Just as science fiction had changed over time, so had the other genres to which the film claimed a relation. *Aliens* is particularly adept at restoring classical aspects of the combat film, aspects that had been very much out of favor since Vietnam made it impossible to presume either victory or fighting on the morally right side:

> Against the backdrop of combat crew crack-ups in *Alien* ... *Aliens* rehabilitated the World War II combat film and, not incidentally, the U.S. military ... yok[ing] science fiction to action adventure and

reflected the military's restoration to public esteem in the Reagan era. The crew of *Aliens* is communal, connected, and combat ready, a unit that would be at home in a World War II combat film. Even the expansion of membership to heretofore marginal groups – blacks, Hispanics, and lesbians – is in line with the progressively open admissions policy of the military squad. The enemy is no longer us – it's them, the creatures in the ventilation ducts and subterranean chambers.

Not that Cameron is a mere jingoist, afflicted with historical amnesia and unfamiliar with the generic transformations of the combat genre since 1945. Appropriately for a tale of posttraumatic stress, *Aliens* owes a good deal of its style and ethos to the Vietnam combat film, the troubled descendent of the World War II prototypes. Led by military incompetents at the service of venal corporate interests, the self-described "grunts," complete with American flag insignia and flamethrowers, reenact a search-and-destroy mission that looks suspiciously like a late-twentieth-century police action. The freak-outs, wild firefights, scrambled video, surly grunts, lower-class ethnicity, macho posturing, even the calculated appropriation of military vernacular, play like a Vietnam-period run-through-the-jungle. Like the military in Vietnam, the marine crew in the film is restricted in the full application of their firepower by rear-echelon motherfuckers ("What are we supposed to use – harsh language?" snaps Hudson.) Like the rumors of war on the home front, the fuzzy news of combat arrives via video footage. Transmitted from cameras in the soldiers' helmets, disjointed flashes of gunfire are watched on monitors from afar by a field commander safely ensconced in an armored personnel carrier. The crosscutting from the real scene of action to the video is fast, furious, and disorienting, the white noise of a television war.[47]

This uneasy coexistence of a Reaganite tone of military recuperation on the one hand and a Vietnam-style borderline visual incoherence on the other has significant implications for the subjectivity of the soldiers. Rendered flesh by their everydayness and group coherence, they are also simultaneously rendered machine, insofar as their vision is disembodied, transmitted back to the personnel carrier to be watched by an audience that is ultimately incapable of doing much to alter the outcome (just like the cinema audience watching the film), such that whatever they may do ultimately has less value than whatever they may see. (See Chapter 3.) Rather than this being strictly Terminator *redux*, it underscores Cameron's deep ambivalence about the very system in which he works. That is, *Aliens* makes very clear that these "grunts" are not fighting in the service of American (implied: democratic) ideology, however much they may bear its symbols. They are instead fundamentally in the corporate employ, an entity that exists entirely for profit. Given the extent to which military operations in the Second Gulf War are in fact carried out by private, contracted corporate agents, the muddy and (for the grunts) fatal line between the Military and the Corporate in *Aliens* was prescient indeed. Cameron's ambivalence about working in a corporate structure does not extend to the military. As Doherty suggests, "*Aliens* also takes as a matter of course the U.S. military's subservience, though ultimate moral superiority, to the company store . . . [I]t is the corporate civilian and not the military professional for whom the film reserves its deepest hatred."[48]

If Doherty suggested the inherent conservatism of *Aliens* without necessarily ascribing that conservatism to Cameron himself, Tim Blackmore has aggressively argued against what he feels is a widespread and incorrect assessment of Cameron's personal conservatism as seen in the film.[49] Blackmore's attack is two-pronged: first, the all but universal account of the film as gynophobic and patriarchal is misguided; second (and extending from the first), this misguided criticism is a function of the "propriety and power of critics in the academic world who feel it is their job to save us from our poor cultural habits."[50]

Blackmore finds the dominant feminist and political readings (many cited above) of *Aliens* to be fundamentally misguided precisely because they take the films to be only symptomatic, and seldom, if ever, look to Cameron or his cast and crew to locate their intentions as interpretive guidelines. Were they to do so, they would find, according to Blackmore, that a populist discourse about Vietnam is far more important in the film than any (psycho-)sexual discourse. To point to just one of the many tropes of the feminist critique at issue: the Alien Queen's nest, which takes on the proportions of a living, breathing body has been read as a gynecological landscape, and a landscape of death and terror. Syllogistically, this has lead to the claims of gynophobia, and the implication that any woman who can survive in this realm can only do so by subscribing to patriarchal ideologies, no matter how heroically she behaves. In fact it may have more in common with the alien jungles, forests and other landscapes in Vietnam that so disoriented U.S. soldiers and all but eviscerated their advantage of superior firepower (also something the Marines have in *Aliens*). Centrally, Blackmore is concerned that the director's version of *Aliens*, in which it is explicitly given to the spectator that Ripley was married and had a child, and, as the result of the events in the first *Alien*, returned to Earth long after that child had lived a full life and died, is not the one up for analysis. If it were, the patriarchal and gynophobic readings simply would not, for Blackmore, obtain. While that is certainly a matter of opinion, Blackmore's insistence on the director's as the definitive version raises a vital question: when a film has a director's cut (or other version), what is the critic's responsibility, what should be her methodology, in considering competing articulations of the film, especially when the "definitive" version may not be the one that either critics or popular audiences saw? Here Blackmore may be accused of the very elitism he claims for other critics: privileging Cameron's director's cut may restore original intent to the interpretation (and intent brings its own lures and snares to the analytical project), but, initially, it was a format available only to the sector of the population who could afford to own laserdisc players and laserdiscs, a technology proportionately far more expensive than DVD is now.

The populist stakes of the second strand of the debate that Blackmore rehearses foreshadow the fiery debate that took place between *Los Angeles Times* film critic Kenneth Turan and James Cameron himself after Turan panned *Titanic* (see Appendix 1 below). The issues are similar: Blackmore excoriates academic critics (though he is himself one) for taking an elitist and more knowing position than the spectators who flocked to the film in droves, all but suggesting the critics saw it from a literally different place, like the safety of the balcony, away from the riff-raff. (In a Cultural Studies mode, this is exactly the dilemma that Sharon Willis takes on. See above.) "The real issue is the importance of the popular, which must be interpreted, not condemned, examined, not judged, read, and not burned; then the popular must be returned to those who chose it: the people."[51] One might well ask whether "the people" who chose Leni Riefenstahl in Hitler's Germany should likewise be given such pride of place. Nevertheless, Blackmore's emphasis on the active readership unique in film to serials and sequels is a point well taken. "What differentiates serial films from others is not just that they are closed syntagmatically and opened paradigmatically, but that they provide space for, and invite the participation of, the reader-viewer."[52] That is, just as every other aforementioned critic who has read the entire series has implied, no element of the series is likely to be read in a vacuum, whether the viewer has actually seen the previous installments or not (and in this case, far more people have seen Cameron's installment than any other), and spectatorial evaluation, whether at the academic or the popular level, will proceed with seriality as one of its vital givens.

THE ABYSS AND THE QUESTION OF CAMERON'S SUBMERGED LEFTISM

If Blackmore felt the need to rescue Cameron from the clutches of feminist elitists, who saw conservative ideology where, to him, there was none, Joe Abbott regards the filmmaker as far more ideologically mobile. He suggests that Cameron's films followed a pattern elucidated by Peter Biskind regarding radical science fiction films of the 1950s, in which, unlike centrist sci-fi, the center was the "Them," and the margin, or radical position, was the "Us." And Abbott argues that the radical "Us" in Cameron films has been, by turns, right-wing and left-ist. In spite of a post-1960s shift to the right in the United States political climate, Abbott proposes that, "the basic utilitarian assumptions granting the needs and desires of the Community at the expense of the Individual (if need be) still form the basis of America's centrist ideology. It is therefore necessary that any political stance aligning itself with radical philosophies must lay bare any inherent malevolence informing this kind of social ethic."[53] And this, for Abbott, is what Cameron's science fiction films do. But they do not always do it from the same position.

The Terminator is for Abbott, as for most other film scholars, a fairly standard right-wing attack on the center. The institutions designed to protect average citizens, symbolized here by the police, are helpless against the cyborg, and it is only when Sarah Connor repudiates the centrist ideology held within these structures, instead adopting a hard Individualist (read: rightist), even survivalist line that Humanity can be saved. Aliens likewise critiques the center from the right, as the Marines prove ineffective, the Corporation proves insidious, and the Individual (Ripley this time) must flex her individuality to save what's left of the Community (here defined, as so many have noted, by an ad hoc family – in this recalling some of the Western genre's more stripped down scenarios, such as John Ford's The Searchers (1956)). But The Abyss attacks the center from the left. This made the film unique among Cameron's oeuvre, and, as it was at the time his most recent film, seemed at the time to point the way to a political shift in the director – not one necessarily born out by True Lies, but arguably by Titanic (see below).

"The Abyss depicts a breakdown within the corporate apparatus (the rigging crew) and management (the shirts-and-ties that offer a purely sycophantic allegiance to ambiguous executive authorities)."[54] As Doherty suggested of Aliens, Abbott implies a generic hybridity in The Abyss, as it combines political thriller, adventure film, fantasy film, and, of course, science fiction, and all parts of this hybrid product "exhibit left-wing tendencies."[55]

A centrist film would have resolved the white-collar/blue-collar rupture by having management succeed in rescuing its stranded crew, thus valorizing the corporate elite. Such a denouement could have fit easily into *The Abyss*'s narrative (the rescue, after all, does not take place until the storm has passed and rescue procedures are getting underway). But by preferring to have the non-terrestrials save the day, the film allies itself with the left, refusing to glorify in any way the upper levels of the corporate apparatus. Although *The Abyss*'s basis for opposing the center is quite different from that proposed in *The Terminator*, the point here is that by refusing to valorize the institution(s) representing America's ideological center, both films take an equally radical stance to censure what they depict as a deteriorating sociopolitical infrastructure.[56]

No ideological articulation is without gaps and inconsistencies, even totalitarian ones, and that Cameron seems to be mounting a critique of centrist corporate culture in *The Abyss* coexists with an absence of a criticism not only of the gender relations inherent in a traditional Western marriage structure, but also of numerous other ideological institutions. For that matter, in spite of its implicit portrait of a single mother (to be), neither does *The Terminator*. These two films made five years apart come from politically opposite positions, the earlier film investing in the primacy of the individual over social and ideological institutions as well as (though for the benefit of) the community, the later film investing in what Abbott calls a "utopian 'not-us' society,"[57] seem to indicate that, whatever Cameron's aims, his films frequently function as the Marxist/structuralist political philosopher Louis Althusser suggested that most cultural production does: made by institutions for constitutive and constituted social subjects – for whom participation in the cinema experience is part of what makes them the subjects they are – films bear political and ideological meaning regardless of what the maker intends.[58]

If Abbott is content to call the political valences of *The Abyss* left wing, James Kendrick goes so far as to label them Marxist. Entering into the realm of Marxist film theory inevitably engages the heart of the uneasy relation between materialist history and popular culture. That is, for Kendrick and others, Marx's predictions about proletarian revolution have not come to pass in significant measure because popular culture, and cinema first and foremost, have produced a kind of ideological stupefaction in this same body, a new opiate of the masses. Even the 1960s, the decade of American protest movements, was marked by a post-studio cinema that was, as Robert Ray put it, "superficially radical, internally conservative."[59] It is Kendrick's contention that, conversely, "films like *The Abyss*, *Aliens* and *Titanic* are, in fact, superficially conservative, internally radical."[60] This reversal is in part enabled by the generic flexibility and hybridity also noted by so many other critics as typical of Cameron films, such that the conventions of any one genre neither adhere exclusively nor dominate, and this, for Kendrick, opens up a way to read "the power struggle between class-representational characters [that] is so strong in Cameron's films that it can almost be considered the defining characteristic of his work."[61] In *Aliens*, Kendrick sees Cameron's Marxist class struggle in the vilification of Company man Carter Burke and his willingness to treat the workers (Marines) as disposable assets in order to bring profit (the alien embryo stashed inside any one of them) to the corporation. In *Titanic* class struggle is clearly delineated not just by Jack's working-class hero, but also, even more, by the very geography of the ship itself, with its first-, second- and third-class decks, each determining the fate of its passengers.

In *The Abyss*, it is the Everyman hero Bud Brigman (Ed Harris) who is the pivotal character. Unlike his antagonist, Lieutenant Hiram Coffey (Michael Biehn), he moves easily among the oilrig workers, never commanding them as Coffey does with little success, but always asking them to carry out the required tasks. That it is an anti-nuclear film (as is *Terminator 2*), made just before the end of the Cold War and the Reagan Era, produces an intimacy between the military and the corporate.

> *The Abyss* posits a somewhat ambiguous class structure that is assembled of the working class, the capitalists, and the military. In

this film, the military appears to control the capitalist system while being, at the same time, an extension of it. The capitalist business-men of Benthic Petroleum, represented by the weak and ineffectual Gerald Kirkhill (Ken Jenkins), at first seem to be used at the whim of the military-industrial complex represented by Lieutenant Coffey. However, when viewed from the standpoint that men like Coffey risk their lives protecting the United States from the Soviet Union, thus preserving the capitalist system enjoyed by men like Kirkhill, it is, in fact, the military that is being used by the capitalists. Either way, they exist in a symbiotic relationship in *The Abyss* and can be viewed as two heads of the same creature.[62]

If Kendrick sees an ideological consistency in Cameron that Abbott does not, then, following Thomas Doherty's analysis of Cameron's positioning of the Marines and the Company in *Aliens*, there might seem to be no "either way." But that the corporate capitalist structure is using the military for ends that confuse ideology and profit is certainly not in doubt. As Blackmore does, Kendrick privileges the director's cut of *The Abyss* and *Aliens* (*Titanic* not having an alternate version), again posing the very open question of whether, in order to make Marxist claims, or any other claims touching on class-struggle, one is obligated to use the version accessible to the greatest number of viewers (read: classes).

THE *TITANIC* PHENOMENON

It will come as no surprise to anyone that the single film that has gen-erated the most attention in Cameron's career is *Titanic*, currently the most profitable film of all time, and, until recently, also the most expensive (Peter Jackson's *King Kong* (2005) now holds the record by a slim (3½%) margin at $207 million).[63] Given the hype surrounding the film's production – especially its budget – it was almost compul-sory for film critics to weigh in, often repeatedly (see below). But it is also a film to which numerous scholars have turned to attempt to describe what its popularity meant in cultural, historical and political terms, to say nothing of what it might signal for industrial shifts in Hollywood.

Very few movies have entire anthologies of scholarly work devoted to them, and usually this comes after many years, typically decades, when the dust of history has begun to settle on the films, and they have been safely lodged in the canon of cinema classics.[64] Titanic, a dramatization of the events that led to the sinking of the world's largest ship, part romance, part action film, part historical drama, was sui generis, and within two years of the film's release, an essay collection, Titanic: Anatomy of a Blockbuster, emerged that asked a range of questions that only seemed obvious because the film was already approaching the $2 billion mark at the global box office: "Why has Titanic become so popular?" The volume's editors wanted to know "Why has this film become a cultural and film phenomenon? What makes it so fascinating to the film-going public?"[65] That the film was a blockbuster was a given by its astronomical profit (as well as its astronomical outlay; see my Introduction to this volume). But that it needed anatomization, as the collection's title suggested, spoke to its unique nature. Were this Terminator 3 directed by Cameron (which ultimately was made with another screenwriter and director), the film's blockbuster status would seem to need no analysis – loud, high-tech movies with time-bending plots, non- and superhuman characters, and the fate of the world or even the universe hanging in the balance are par for the course at the top of the box office lists, as Star Wars (1977), Lord of the Rings (2001), and Spider-Man (2002) make clear. But Titanic went against so much conventional wisdom, or seemed to, that critics and scholars alike almost immediately began to examine it, the man, the industrial system and culture that had produced it, and the social groupings that so enthusiastically received it. Gaylyn Studlar and Kevin Sandler suggested that Titanic's broad appeal rendered it a particularly "open text," in spite and perhaps because of conflicting individual interpretations. Whether the film was aesthetically and historically significant or simply very expensive and profitable schlock, in this most scholars could agree:

> *Titanic* is significant because of its popularity, and that popularity is a
> very complicated matter. It appears dependent on contemporary cul-
> ture, on perceptions of history, on patterns of consumerism and glo-
> balization, as well as on those elements experienced filmgoers
> conventionally expect of juggernaut film events in the 1990s – awe-
> some screen spectacle, expansive action, and, more rarely seen,
> engaging characters and epic drama. *Titanic* cannot be approached
> without an appreciation of the need to make sense of this film … as
> an important aspect of contemporary culture.[66]

That a collection could be put together and brought out so quickly in the
generally glacial context of academic publishing also suggested the
dizzying speed with which the events spooling out from *Titanic*'s release
had happened. It is a conceit that one of the symptoms of modern life
is its velocity, but *Titanic* seemed to offer a case study like none anyone
had seen, not only for its volume but for its rapidity and its directness.

The obvious central detail, statistic and proof of the *Titanic* phenomenon is, of course, its box-office figures. Here it is useful to recall
what films *Titanic* beat to break first the U.S. and then the international
records. They were, respectively, *Star Wars* and *Jurassic Park* (1993), both
science fiction/action/adventure films. If *Titanic* could be considered
either action or adventure, then because it blended historical romance,
melodrama and disaster film, the nature of those designations was rendered distinct. *Titanic* may exhibit generic hybridity, as do Cameron's
other films, but the genres come in sequence: a modern day 20-minute
preamble is followed by an 80-minute sequence that is all about Rose
and Jack's love story, followed by 90 minutes of action as the ship hits
the iceberg and sinks. For Peter Kramer, an adjunct of that distinction
was *Titanic*'s privileging of a female audience without alienating the
crucial male audience – something he contends Cameron has done
with success in the past.[67] Anomalous as it was in the blockbuster fir-
mament, the film triumphed not least because it actively did two
things: "the marketing and the film itself … engage[d] audiences,
with an emphasis on the role played in this process by love, the act of

story-telling, and female subjectivity. . . . the film (supported by the surrounding publicity) explains itself to its audiences, offering them guidance on how to understand and enjoy *Titanic*."[68] Every film comes loaded with cues to the spectator, some generically specific, some based on star intertexts, some on director expectations, as well as other cues. For Kramer, *Titanic* exceeded even these protocols, but it was not unprecedented. He credits Cameron for making the female action-adventure heroine acceptable to both female and male audiences, and charts the rise of blockbusters with women at their subjective center – not only Cameron's own (*The Terminator*, *Aliens* and T2), but those of others as well, such as *Demolition Man* (1993) and *Speed* (1994, both starring Sandra Bullock), *Twister* (1996, Helen Hunt) and *Contact* (1997, Jodie Foster). And in most of these cases, these female stars were the emotional center of each film.

It must be said that Kramer's critique takes *Titanic*'s emotional register at its declarative value, and is content with eternalities of love that are rendered so by Jack's death – thus they are "together forever, at least in [Rose's] heart."[69] Kramer's exhaustive accounting of the generic components of *Titanic* includes melodrama, whose romantic rendition contains the emotional center of the film. Through this rubric it's possible to see one particularly Cameronian combination of outright originality in his technical work, and very canny reference to a set of film images (and not images Kramer singles out): the scene in which Jack and Rose are discovered having just made love in the back of a car in the cargo hold hearkens directly back to an almost identical, class-crossed "lovers discovered" scene in another melodrama, *Now, Voyager* (1941), whose narrative arc involves the awakening of an upper-class young woman (Bette Davis's Charlotte Vale), a repressive mother, and a conclusion in which romantic love is refused for something else (in that case motherhood rather than global adventure). But where in *Now, Voyager* romantic love is sacrificed for maternal love – and is therefore explicitly rendered precious in its trade value, for Kramer, romantic love in *Titanic* occupies a far less certain valence, one represented in the setting of the film itself. The eponymous ship is simultaneously the place where Rose meets Jack, but also, and first, the "slave ship," as Rose calls it, "taking me back to America in chains." Kramer suggests that Titanic's success with women turns on a deft combination of acknowledging a collective ambivalence with the stakes of romantic love, and, after establishing the story as being told by underwater explorer Brock Lovett (Bill Paxton), ceding control of the narrative to a woman, Rose DeWitt Bukater (Gloria Stuart):

> [R]omantic love is shown to be a force potentially as deadly as the icy water, but it is also portrayed as a life-giving force, which gives back to Rose a will to live that she had abandoned when the two lovers first met, and, more precisely, the will and confidence to live her own life, unrestrained by the social conventions of the day. When Rose decides to save herself, the potentially deadly selflessness of a woman's romantic love is transformed into the selfishness of her love of life. Perhaps there is a price to pay for this salvation. When the present-day Rose talks about the guilt of the survivors looking for redemption without ever finding it, she may also be referring to herself … After all, Jack has to die and their romantic pact had to be broken for Rose to be able to live … Behind the romantic dream of an adolescent girl lurks the nightmare of suppressed female rage. Rose's story is also a cautionary tale about the destructive power women may unleash on an oppressive patriarchal order.[70]

Because Cameron remains ever in command of the filmmaking process, he is also free to take the unusual step of describing his own shifts in thinking from the beginning of his own engagement with the Titanic process. If the central character of a film often stands in for the director, here Kramer suggests that Cameron's stand-in, Brock Lovett, starts as the central figure who controls the diegesis, but is quickly, and eventually willingly, supplanted by the older Rose. Like Cameron,

> Lovett can be seen as … another man obsessed with the Titanic who did go down to see and film the wreck and a filmic story-teller who

takes command of complex technology to achieve his goal. What happens in the prologue is the undercutting of Cameron's position, first by the [snarky] comments of Lovett's assistant, then, more importantly, by his reluctant handing over of the role of story-teller to Rose. It is as if Cameron declared that this story and this film belonged to the woman on the screen, and also by implication, to the women in the audience.[71]

Kramer is hardly the only writer who marks the ambivalence of love and romance in *Titanic*. Kramer's essay title began "Women First." *The Nation* columnist Katha Pollitt's essay on a similar topic was called "Women and Children First,"[72] and the children at issue were young girls. Pollitt noted *Titanic's* success with no small satisfaction, claiming that it represented a strand of "romantic feminism" that flew in the face of the "complacent moralizing and conservative claptrap [of] fundamentalist Christians who think women want to be ordered around by dishwashing good old boys."[73] While the film drew on some of the familiar codes of Hollywood women's pictures from the 1930s and 1940s, Pollitt saw a crucial difference:

[I]t's a three-hankie romance centered on the female character, with tons of glamour and gorgeous clothes. But unlike any women's pictures of recent years I can think of, the heroine does not have to choose between work and love or solitude and compromise. She does not have a violent husband, a fatal illness, a shaved head, a kidnapped child. She is not punished for being sexual — no back-alley abortion, stalker, AIDS, rape. She is not a perky sidekick or a long-suffering, tired-looking wife. We are not asked to believe that she would find Woody Allen attractive or enjoy being a prostitute even for a night.[74]

Feminism — and broader social critique — though this might have been, it was, for Pollitt, Hollywood feminism, with all its compromises and conventions.

Cameron's movie is more of a poetic meditation on class and gender and even, in its all-whiteness, race: The sinking of Titanic represents the onrushing destruction of the old order, in which a rapacious, cruel and secretly sordid upper class suppresses proletarian and immigrant vigor and sells its own daughters into genteel bondage. It's hokum, of course; Cameron barely individualizes the steerage passengers he champions, and … underplays the disproportionate death toll of steerage passengers and crew members. This is a pro-democracy movie, perhaps, in the sense that Diana was the people's princess …

Through [Jack, Rose] discovers herself as a sexual being and free spirit, abandons fiancé, mother, class for … a long and exciting life as an actress, aviatrix, traveler, potter, mother. Fifteen hundred people perish in torment, but this is a movie with a happy ending and an optimistic vision of history. The twentieth century, which for so many men is a saga of loss, decline and displacement, has told a different story to women.[75]

Vitally, the critical register of Titanic can never be divorced from its Hollywood context, but that does not obviate either critique or its context. One implication of Pollitt's analysis is that, given the popular and populist modes of Hollywood blockbuster storytelling, there may be a limited number of ways to articulate any kind of feminism at all, and that, by its very nature, it will be a complex and ambivalent one.

Pollitt's proposed relation between Titanic and Diana, who died in a car accident the same year Cameron's film was released, is illuminating, and she is not alone in having made that connection. Robert von Dassanowsky elaborates on the similarity between the worldwide mourning of the former Princess of Wales and the global blockbuster.[76] He was particularly struck by the comparisons each entity evoked. So laden with a particular form of postmodern nostalgia, a semi-serious and slightly undefined desire to return to something (but in a form neither had ever actually embodied), was each, that it further strengthened their bond in a specific cultural moment:

Just as the late princess has been compared with everyone from Marilyn Monroe to Mother Teresa, [*Titanic*] has been ranked alongside *Gone with the Wind* (1939) in a field of overused superlatives. On reflection, *Titanic* will no doubt be viewed as a collection of reused parts that amount to far more than the politically correct whole. For rather than stating something "new," *Titanic* is a revisitation of sociocultural and cinematic statements concerned with the alienation brought on by the simultaneously positive and negative modernism of the twentieth century.

The parables of the Lady and the Ship – Princess Diana's death and James Cameron's *Titanic* – appear to have filled the need for mass ritual and emotional fulfillment in a period of relative aimlessness: the ideological vacuum of post-Cold War civilization, heightened by fin-de-siècle panic and by what Umberto Eco calls a postmodern "crisis of reason." Both parables focus on an icon of the repressed woman in a period when feminism has faded from popular thought and pundits claim that a "feminized" world has already taken root or sexuality is no longer an issue. Nevertheless, these reactions to the power, cynicism, even negativity of the impersonal cyber-virtual world of the 1990s are themselves illusory: Princess Diana was nothing less than a shrewd manipulator of the image she helped cultivate with the international media, and *Titanic* is less a film of narrative originality than one of cutting-edge technological entertainment. Both were created with such media savvy as to almost belie their messages.[77]

Like Kramer, von Dassanowsky suggests that, rather than renovating the media landscape entirely, *Titanic* (and Princess Diana) worked with that landscape to teach postmodern subjects precisely how to consume the nostalgia on offer. In the case of the blockbuster, this involved Cameron's adoption of an "ersatz female gaze."[78] This gaze presents an easy and identificatory viewing position for the female spectator, one that is welcoming, but, in terms of its historical positioning, false. "A class-based society, as suggested through Diana's persona or *Titanic*'s set pieces, despite its rabid inequality, also offers escapism, albeit a retrograde one, from the dumbing down of today's socioculture with its faceless barcodes and vague email identities."[79] If, even before her death, Diana's life took on cinematic proportions, *Titanic* is a film that takes on the proportions of lived experience, and for similar reasons. Each scenario offers up to women – particularly young women – a defense of female equality raised to mythic and spectacular proportions. Indeed, the mythic content of a liberation narrative is both aided by and struggles with (and against) its spectacular form. Von Dassanowsky concludes that *Titanic* underscores

> ... a contradictory postmodern Zeitgiest. The fantasy of Rose and the twin mountains of ice and iron, like that of Princess Diana, enables women to identify with, and deify, the struggle for female ascendancy in the past that suggests the stasis of that development in Western society in the present. The patriarchal, male-oriented anxiety underpinning Eco's "crisis of reason" and the possibility of female revolt/authority are exploited in *Titanic* as well, and it is a far greater revelation. Caledon and Jack find an uncontrollable nature, a defeated/ing modernity (this from a film and filmmaker associated with cutting edge virtual-effects technology), and together they signal the "feminization" that will be needed to survive and understand the death of patriarchal modernisms.[80]

For some, however, the brilliance of *Titanic* lay precisely in how Cameron was able to bypass modern *and* postmodern circuitry altogether in favor an overt ethic of sentimentality that hearkened back to classical Hollywood.[81] Todd F. Davis and Kenneth Womack argue that "by deliberately adopting the stylistics of sentimentality in his screenplay, Cameron recalls yet another, less cynical time in *Titanic*. As with the golden age of Hollywood musicals or the 1950s-era films of Doris Day and Rock Hudson, *Titanic* eschews the irony of modernity and the narrative dislocation of postmodernity in favor of yet another, more sentimentalized genre in which good inevitably wins out over evil, heroes invariably overcome class barriers, and lovers always find the means to endure despite harrowing odds."[82] Indeed, that the film was so unironic, so located, so sentimental, was the central reason that academics and other members of the intelligentsia could not credit *Titanic* with cinematic greatness. This struck Davis and Womack as itself ironic, if not hypocritical, since the high–low art distinction was precisely that which was supposed to have broken down under postmodern conditions – yet here remained those very same critics, reinstating the boundary because *Titanic* was not in the "correct" mood or mode:

> In sharp contrast to modern or postmodern cinema – steeped, as they are, in cynicism and intentionally vague in terms of heroes and villains, right and wrong – Cameron's film requires us to check our poststructuralist skepticism at the door and accept his deliberately sentimentalized narrative at face value. Yet Cameron perceptively recognizes the cultural hurdles inherent in such a transaction: How can a late twentieth-century writer and director convince an ethically jaded contemporary audience to embrace a class-defying love affair complete with a cardboard Edwardian villain? Cameron achieves this awkward cultural transformation through a variety of narrative means. The ship itself – literally a character in Cameron's screenplay that exerts as much narrative force as either of the film's protagonists – provides the audience with a cultural referent of tremendous import. The mere mention of *Titanic*'s disaster narrative is enough to conjure up a powerful form of shared nostalgia for an era that most of us scarcely even know.[83]

"A powerful form of shared nostalgia for an era that most of us scarcely even know," would seem to be the very definition of one aspect of postmodernism.[84] Still, the ship, combined with the time-shifting narrative framing device that seems to transport the spectator back to a time (the Edwardian Era) when such sentimentality and sincerity might be seen without quotation marks, are vital in producing for the spectator an ethical register of viewing that permits this non-ironic position in a wholly ironic and indeterminate world – hence, for Davis and Womack, the success of *Titanic* has less to do with the special effects and more to do with the emotional *loci* to which viewers have access, over and over, if they like.

Whether it is possible to go back in such an untrammeled way to a sincere and sentimental mode is debatable; less so is Cameron's desire to do so, a desire that certainly stems from some form of nostalgia, though whether it's of the nature Davis and Womack suggest or not is another matter. But the desire is not simply aesthetic, nor is it simply cultural, however much it is coded by Cameron and read by critics in those terms. Intimately bound up in both of these rubrics is the issue of economics – specifically how and by whom Hollywood film is now financed. Studios are no longer the personality-driven (for better or worse), venerated dream factories of the classical period, but late capitalist subsidiaries of multinational corporations whose drive to satisfy shareholders, it is often argued, has definitively tilted the balance of what comes out of Paramount, MGM, Universal, and 20th Century Fox (or what's left of them) towards product over art, spectacle over narrative. Furthermore, the product at issue has profit potential far exceeding the single or multiple viewings any spectator could traditionally have experienced at the picture shows of days past. Now, cinema has replicated itself, morphing (not unlike like the T1000 in Cameron's *T2*) into other media: video and DVD to be rented or owned, as well as other commodity tie-ins. This, as I have argued in the introduction, is a crucial aspect of blockbuster culture. To be sure, the increased tension between film as product and film as artistic utterance is as easy to see in *Titanic* as anywhere. That Cameron might be symptomatic of that struggle seems to be astutely summed up by Fox chairman Bill Mechanic's oxymoronic comment that the studio was co-funding Cameron's "$200 million art film."

For James Hurley, this is the place to begin teasing out the allegorical status of *Titanic*, a film he regards, following Mechanic, as a "blockbuster art film."[85] "*Titanic* allegorizes the effects of the transition into this new economic and mediatic regime on the aesthetic status of

Hollywood cinema, and, more precisely, the allegorical staging in Cameron's blockbuster of an institutional struggle to reconcile economic with cultural capital."[86] The industrial specifics of the transition underlying Hurley's analysis are these: starting in the post-war period, American film audiences were offered an alternative to Hollywood cinema in the form of art cinema (e.g., Ingmar Bergman, Akira Kurosawa, Satyajit Ray, Jean-Luc Godard). These films, offering a certain (arguably) modernist psychological interiority, narrative indeterminacy, and emphasis on (rather than effacement of) the relation of content to form, thrive for some decades and develop and maintain a particularly educated and affluent audience, whose affluence might be expressed in cultural rather than economic terms.[87] As the dominant mode of American cinema becomes an early form of the current blockbuster (*Star Wars*, *Jaws*), art cinema diminishes as a force in the U.S. But it is replaced by two other fields of moving image production, American Independent cinema (e.g., Spike Lee, Jim Jarmusch, David Lynch), and the heritage drama – the sort of film most likely to be made by Merchant/Ivory or broadcast on PBS or A&E. Hurley contends that Cameron is acutely aware of these developments, and, in his public rhetoric about the necessity of cutting-edge technology to bring about historical accuracy, positions *Titanic* to be legible to both the current blockbuster *and* art-house audiences – audiences that are typically not expected at the same screening.

The contentious nature of that rhetoric obtains in the film as well, particularly in the colliding discourses about art and taste – exactly what a $200 million dollar art film must have if that sector of its audience is to excuse its budget, see it as something necessary rather than wasteful (and therefore attend the picture at all, to say nothing of repeatedly). Cal derides Rose's purchase (with his money) of Picassos and Degas, saying to their maid that Picasso "won't amount to a thing." Here, Hurley notes, the audience invariably and inevitably laughs, easily seeing Cal as anachronistic, unable to see the future as Rose and Jack (an artist himself, though hardly of Picasso's modernist bent) do. Anachronism soon becomes synonymous with villainy. There's more to it, though, and Hurley points out the paradox of taking historical license with (works of) art in a film that made bold claims to historical authenticity, singling out "Rose's impossible collection of paintings – by Monet, Cezanne, Degas, and (inevitably) Picasso – which signals her 'progressive thinking' to an audience able to recognize these artworks and respond to them *precisely because they were never in fact there*, these paintings end up not several miles below the surface of the North Atlantic, but as 'timeless classics' in some of the world's great museums."[88] The *Titanic* becomes a kind of impossible museum, but in employing this paradoxical strategy, *Titanic* lays claim to itself as a similarly timeless classic.

Nevertheless, the film with aspirations to timeless classicism also has affinities with a baser genre than historical drama: melodrama, and by extension, Hurley suggests Cameron shares affinities with Douglas Sirk, Vincente Minelli and Nicholas Ray, some of the more politically inscriptive directors of the genre. Recalling Cameron's (joking) statement that the film's politics stop "just short of Marxist dogma,"[89] the pivotal figure in this melodrama might not be the female lead, as it usually is, but Jack Dawson, the proletarian artist. It's this dual identity that is so crucial to *Titanic*'s possible political readings – where it stands on the issue of class and class struggle. Rose is drawn to both parts of Jack's identity, but, intellectually and emotionally, they meet on the field of art and culture. Yet her taste (Picasso, etc.) and his practice (a mimesis that makes no challenge whatsoever to spatio-temporal continuity) are not only different, but also at odds. Rose's is surely the more progressive aesthetic in 1912, the film's diegetic time. But at the moment of *Titanic*'s release, Jack may be the figure who most represents the audience's conditions of subjectivity. As Hurley writes:

> [W]hat gives Jack his contemporaneity is his *dissociation* from precisely this [modernist] aesthetic movement and mode. Although we can see Jack as neither modernist nor traditional realist, it is not inappropriate at all to see him as untimely *postmodernist*, the photographic mimicry performed by his drawings now no longer to be

considered that which gives evidentiary grounding, but, indeed, exactly the opposite, as reproduction layered on reproduction, thus exemplifying what we know through the Baudrillardian axiom as the "precession of the simulacra."[90]

That a pre-modernist artist living in modern times could come to signify the spectator's postmodern conditions suggests just how slippery signification in Titanic really is. As anomalous as the film remains on many levels, it nevertheless has much to say about the current state of the Hollywood machine. Hurley concludes,

[T]he ability of the New Hollywood post-digital image to morph itself into (virtually!) anything and everything, so that in some inevitable sense it is always already deconstructed, means not only has it forfeited any claims it might want to make for the historical or ontological reliability of that which it presents (no matter what stark trace of the real it may purport to represent), but that its internal image-logic is now in transparent alignment with the logic of the commodity, the image no longer able to make even a pretense of possessing the value that goes beyond the immediate terms of each act of its exchange ... The appeals Titanic makes through its museum imagination to the auraticized aesthetic object are then especially crucial, for they allow the film to figure itself as operating in a space where "the economy of the world has been reversed," even, of course, while placing itself as fully as it can into that world's circuit of commodity exchange.[91]

Running through Hurley's critique of Titanic's uneasy relation to capital and taste is a canny understanding of Titanic as a heritage film, largely informed by Julian Stringer's account in his essay "'The China Had Never Been Used!': On the Patina of Perfect Images in Titanic."[92] In it, Stringer suggests that Titanic's massive popularity hinges on its ability to fuse protocols of the very American blockbuster with those of the European, and specifically British, heritage film. Heritage films, as

Stringer has it, are works whose "stunning art and production design [reflect] a style of popular filmmaking obsessed with looking back and recreating the past in all its glory and nostalgic perfection."[93] That these films had a high-toned aesthetic did not stop them from making money; if they were not blockbusters, films from the same period as *Titanic* like *Howard's End* and *Orlando* (both 1992), *Age of Innocence* and *The Remains of the Day* (both 1993), *Sense and Sensibility* (1996), *Amistad* and *Mrs. Dalloway* (both 1997), were both critically lauded and profitable.

For Stringer, *Titanic*, while clearly marked by the combined Anglo-American sensibilities of the blockbuster and the heritage film, exceeded such national markings – it had to, or else it could not have succeeded on the international scale it did. "Combining the wizardry of technological spectacle with pristine heritage visuals," he argues, "the film looks back to the early twentieth century in a manner that speaks to the uses to which the past is put in all modern capitalist and consumer societies."[94] And central to spectators anywhere in the world recognizing what is in front of them, when presented with *Titanic*, is an understanding of the patina of objects – the china, the sheets, the famous Heart of the Ocean diamond (all thought to be languishing, decades later, on the ocean floor, separated from their owners and users) – in which "age comes to signify cultural status,"[95] as one of the central – and malleable – ingredients of heritage film, even in its block-buster form. Stringer points to the film's double narrative, its framing device which contains the historical drama neatly within, as one key to its success:

> It is rare for such a popular example of the heritage genre to oscillate between two temporal frameworks. [S]uch flexibility in terms of how a story can be told might undermine the perceived authenticity of the past being created. More usually, heritage filmmakers immerse the viewer in a complete, because unified and single-layered, nostalgic illusion. [Yet Cameron's] double diegesis cannot exactly be said to constitute a rupture, either. Hollywood's 1997 version of events on the *Titanic* nowhere explores historical contradiction,

nowhere provides analytic comparison. Yet this flaw in ideological critique has the effect of opening up the film's reception possibilities a little more. Paradoxically, by drawing such clear distinctions between the old and the new, between the pristine and the decrepit, *Titanic* passes over historical contradictions but heightens emotional investment.

... Cameron's use of a double temporal framework does recognize ... patina's function as a system of mediation. Relations between the past and the present, then and now, the living and the dead, are filtered through the symbolic cultural properties associated with old physical objects. Material culture acts as a "bridge" to the feelings and sentiments we choose to unload on the past. ... [W]hat symbolic properties do we inherit from those objects, what cultural values do we now invest in them, and who are "we" anyway? In the world of transnational capital and commerce, portrayals of elites, as well as conservative visions of a vague and ambivalently signaled national past, are helped along by the patina system. For whatever elite lifestyles are threatened, new social claims will need to be verified, new questions of inheritance and social status will require legitimation.

Rather than an inevitable hegemonic relation to *Titanic*'s images and narrative (something I would argue is still altogether likely, if hardly the sole possibility), an international audience in late consumer capitalism has other options that have precisely to do with the increasingly muddled line between spectator (and consumer) of a film, and consumer of the objects surrounding the film (copies of the china, the Heart of the Ocean, actual objects from *Titanic*'s Rosarito, Mexico set) — objects that take on a kind of instant patina. So the film's international triumph touches on the film's ability to create a false, and altogether consumable, nostalgia. "The film teaches viewers to miss things they have never actually been denied . . . Instead of expecting viewers to supply lived memories, they are now encouraged to bring nostalgia to an image that will supply the memory of a loss never suffered. As such, *Titanic* represents nostalgia without lived experience or collective historical memory."[96] All of which is to say that *Titanic* is particularly adept at commodifying history, and replacing a relation to historical discourse with the experience of an historical spectacle.[97]

Vivian Sobchack likewise considers the framing story crucial to the intense effect *Titanic* had on its audiences. Sobchack boils down the vast number of viewer responses to the film, as found everywhere from letters to the editor to fan sites to entertainment television interviews in multiplex lobbies and elsewhere, to three kinds: "It's really old fashioned and romantic," "It made me cry," and "It really happened." She asks, "exactly what is the referent of 'it' in these phrases?"[98] Indeed, central to Sobchack's investigation and analysis is the very notion of emotional intensity – the "it" in question. Sobchack sees no need to argue the obvious – that the film is not as historically accurate as it looks, that the script is weak, that it resides in the "low" realm of melodrama as much as it does in action, spectacle and historical recreation, responsible or otherwise. But this is not to say the film is devoid of "poetic power and emotional force" – how can it be, given its record-setting numbers? And this quality arises from two interrelated aspects of the film:

> The first is the absolutely crucial *frame story*, which, set in the present day, narratively encircles the irreversibility of the historical past – reconstituting it in the "roundness" of the film as a whole as a felicitous and comforting "eternal return" that undoes catastrophe and death. The second is the film's particularly *resonant imagery*, which functions as a quite literal "medium of exchange" between the film's two temporal registers of past and present and its two spatial registers of vast and small – and thus allows for their *reversibility*. These two correlated features constitute *Titanic* as perhaps the most deeply felt and yet bathetic disaster movie ever made.[99]

That is, the framing story literally surrounds the past-tense narrative, allowing spectators a safe space (very much like the state-of-the-art bathysphere that gives us access to images of the real Titanic in the film itself, Sobchack notes) in which to have an emotionally intense response to a reenactment of historical events without having to get their feet wet in history itself. What results is a conflation of emotional and historical authenticity – a very historically specific (which is to say, late capitalist) form of utopian nostalgia. Writing more recently about a slew of historically removed, critically acclaimed films that are also politically critical themselves (*Good Night, and Good Luck*, *Capote*, *Brokeback Mountain* (all 2005)), *New York Times* film critic A.O. Scott makes a useful distinction between period and historical films that also implies a distinction between potentially activated viewers, and those who may only think they are. "Watching these movies, with their painstaking detail and their 'trompe l'oeil' leading performances, we may also wonder how we got from there to here, a line of inquiry that the pictures frustrate by means of their elaborate visual fidelity," Scott writes. "The difference between a period film and a historical film, in other words, is that while a historical film implies a continuity with the present, the period film, far more common in Hollywood, seals the past in a celluloid vitrine, establishing a safe distance between then and now."[100]

In Scott's terms via Sobchack, then, *Titanic* is a period film masquerading as an historical one. It is not just the narrative structure that permits this, but a range of specific images and image devices as well. One of the most powerful is the offering up of "genuine" footage of the "real" *Titanic* at the bottom of the Atlantic:

> [L]ooking at the footage of the remains of the ship, we are brought both physically closer to the past and temporally more distant from it. It is precisely this irresolvable paradox presented by the real *Titanic* that becomes poetically grounded in the frame story and generates nostalgic longing for a temporal proximity with the past that is impossible to achieve. And it is precisely this paradox that finds resolution in the film's breathtaking computer graphic dissolves – not only between present and past, but also between the different ontological and epistemological relations we have to what we distinguish as history and fiction.[101]

This device, and the framing narrative in which it is set, then, cordon off history. History is not merely framed, it is contained, no longer of any real significance. Yet that this is the case – and that this might also be perfectly obvious not only to scholars but to some sector of the "civilian" audience ("I know very well, but all the same . . . "), does not stop Sobchack from remaining invested in *Titanic* at the emotional level. Very much as Sharon Willis, when thinking about *Terminator 2*, considered herself no less a part of culture just for being a critic of it, Sobchack understands her critical position not as a replacement for any other position she might take, but as an essential adjunct. "Historically conscious as I am, " she concludes, "I was appalled by *Titanic*; but bourgeois subject that I am (and against my intellectual will and to my shame), I also shed into its collective cinematic bucket a big, wet, nostalgic, and antiquarian tear or two."[102]

A significant portion of scholarship on *Titanic* focuses on Rose and the importance of Cameron having chosen a young, progressive woman to take the audience through the narrative's dramatic events. Her lover, the working-class artist Jack Dawson, tends to be read as a device – as he most certainly is – one employed to free Rose from her arranged marriage, and one that must inevitably be forfeited in the romantic mode of sacrificial love in order that Jack and Rose never come up against the inescapable limitations of their class-crossed union. (Love may conquer all on a ship, sinking or otherwise, but back on land there are bills to pay and social groupings to be shut out of.) To the extent that Jack exists for other purposes (not including the wooing of the teenage girl demographic), he is, as James Hurley notes, a stand-in for James Cameron himself, as well as a sly acknowledgement of the film's postmodern stance (see above). For David Gerstner, Jack not only stands in for Cameron, but in so doing also speaks to a tradition of American realism in the visual arts, which not only obviously predates postmodernism, but also has everything to do with managing discourses of gender and sexuality that circulate in *Titanic*.[103]

Specifically, Jack, as a practitioner of realism, is there to put back in the bottle the dual genies of feminine excess (Rose in control of the narrative) and potential homosexuality (what might come from Jack's androgynous avatar as played by Leonardo DiCaprio and by his avocation to be an "artiste"). But there is another duality at work – one made much of in the publicity surrounding the film, especially by Cameron himself: that of Cameron having rendered the drawings read by *Titanic*'s audience as having been created by Jack. Rose, then, is not only rendered an artistic creation, an image, by Jack's hand (that is really in fact Cameron's hand, not DiCaprio's), she is also rendered image by Cameron's directorial hand (aided and abetted by the performance of Kate Winslet). If the image in the drawing is static (or appears to be at 24 frames per second), Gerstner argues that it nevertheless is in need of training and rehabilitation.

> [T]he roles of the filmmaker ... and fictionalized artists ... are to create the appropriately designed figurehead – the Ideal "mix" of woman and machine – both on the ship itself and on the body of the film's female protagonist. The construction of these ideal feminized bodies effectively demarcates a balanced and functional female form ... [T]he creative commingling of the filmmaker with the film's protagonist illustrates the harmonic juxtaposition of the traditional with the industrial arts. Jack is the painter; James is the filmmaker. The creative conjoining of these two figures celebrates the masculinist dream of Twentieth-century American Realism – an art consistently concerned with the dangers of feminine excess.
>
> The feminine body, the film's work of art, is released from the constraints of aristocratic excess through the guiding hand of the male artist(s) in order to emerge as an Ideal American middle-class woman. It is here than Cameron's authorial hand inserts itself. ... anchor[ing] construction of Rose. The first reconstructed representation of Rose passes through the filter of the nonindustrial arts (sort of a blueprint for the industrial model). Rose is sketched by the artist's hand; her womanly essence is captured through the romanticized version of the traditional artist. But the industrial arts are also conceived in the film as capable of rendering the same gendered essence. Cameron's "camera-stylo"[104] ... demonstrably sets itself the

task of fusing machine and nature in the name of creating a work of art. *Titanic*, through the work of art (the female body), signals the successful and historical alliance between the *idea* of art as unique (Walter Benjamin's "aura") and art as mechanically reproduced. Woman and machine successfully mix through the art of the cinematic enterprise.[105]

The masculinist American Realist project's success depends on the reconfiguration of the female body, as evidenced in the scene in which Jack painstakingly sketches Rose, whose pose is familiar from works of art ranging from Titian's *Venus of Urbino* to Manet's *Olympia*. For Gerstner, "Rose, as the artist's model, is no mere sex object who is lasciviously displayed for perverse observation – she is pure work of art. This tightly edited sequence also draws together . . . the important commingling – *through Cameron's hand* – of auteur, actor, director and work of art (painterly and cinematically). . . . Rose is the body where the American-masculinist dream of the feminine is rewritten through the creative practices of painting and, subsequently, filmmaking."[106] Ultimately, then, as Rose is rendered image (by drawing and film), she is also masculinized, crucially taught by Jack to spit, ride a horse Western rather than sidesaddle, simplify her dress, and a host of other behaviors that involve rejecting the excesses of her class as a way of diminishing those excesses of her gender. Her final success is seen in her jettisoning the Heart of the Ocean, the last trace of that excess (and a trace that has been a fetish object for the duration of the film). This trajectory from feminine excess to masculinist American realism has implications far beyond *Titanic*. As Gerstner concludes: "The Hollywood artist . . . is the Ideal American Realist (the non-artist) because the creative enterprise of the Hollywood film industry seamlessly (or so it seems) merges machine and nature through an industry practice crafted on terms of Realism. The Hollywood director's hand, especially in *Titanic*, fulfills the dream of the American non-artist by embodying the creative principles of the American arts: invention, craftsmanship, technowizardry, and, above all, masculinity."[107]

POPULAR APPENDIX 1: TURAN VS. CAMERON

As an appendix to the critical and academic debates, I include a more literal one that needs little framing or context: the debate between *Los Angeles Times* film critic Kenneth Turan, who offered one of the most prominent critical pans of *Titanic*, and James Cameron, who, unlike most directors with box office success to speak for the film, did not take the criticism lying down. The debate did not remain between the two interlocutors – there was an unusually voluminous reader response as well, with a variety of *Los Angeles Times* readers weighing in on many sides, suggesting the issues at hand were not productively treated simply in pro and con terms.

Contrary to the preponderance of major critics, Turan was disappointed by *Titanic*, and felt the script was particularly weak:

MOVIE REVIEW; 'Titanic' Sinks Again (Spectacularly)

Kenneth Turan

> Cameron ... is after more than oohs and aahs. He's already made "The Terminator" and "Terminator 2"; with "Titanic" he has his eye on "Doctor Zhivago"/"Lawrence of Arabia" territory. But while his intentions are clear, Cameron lacks the skills necessary to pull off his coup. Just as the hubris of headstrong shipbuilders who insisted that the Titanic was unsinkable led to an unparalleled maritime disaster, so Cameron's overweening pride has come unnecessarily close to capsizing this project.
>
> For seeing "Titanic" almost makes you weep in frustration. Not because of the excessive budget, not even because it recalls the unnecessary loss of life in the real 1912 catastrophe ... What really brings on the tears is Cameron's insistence that writing this kind of movie is within his abilities. Not only isn't it, it isn't even close.
>
> Instead, what audiences end up with word-wise is a hackneyed, completely derivative copy of old Hollywood romances, a movie that reeks of phoniness and lacks even minimal originality. Worse than

that, many of the characters … are cliches of such purity they ought to be exhibited in film schools as examples of how not to write for the screen.

It is easy to forget, as you wait for the iceberg to arrive and shake things up, how excellent an idea it was to revisit for modern audiences the sinking of what was the largest moving object ever built. As Steven Biel wrote in "Down With the Old Canoe," a fascinating cultural history of public reaction to the event, "The Titanic disaster begs for resolution – and always resists it."

Finally, after so much time has passed you fear the iceberg has slept through its wake-up call, disaster strikes the ship at 11:50 on the night of April 14. Cameron is truly in his element here, and "Titanic's" closing hour is jammed with the most stirring and impressive sights, from towering walls of water flooding a grand dining room to the enormous ship itself defying belief and going vertical in the water.

These kinds of complex and demanding sequences are handled with so much aplomb it's understandable that the director, who probably considers the script to be the easiest part of his job, not only wants to do it all but also thinks he can. Yet as Cameron sails his lonely craft toward greatness, he should realize he needs to bring a passenger with him. Preferably someone who can write.[108]

Reader response was immediate, voluminous, and split about fifty-fifty on whether Turan's pan was accurate. Those in disagreement with Turan were vociferous. According to one reader who took Turan to task precisely on the issue of writing, "Cameron's a brilliant screenwriter. Turan must not have the ear to hear it. His screenplays are compassionate, thrilling and literate."[109] Another reader offered, "after reading Turan's negative review of "Titanic" … I have no intention of reading any future articles or reviews carrying his byline."[110] Clearly, the disagreement went beyond an opinion about a movie. It often touched on the public perception of the role of the film critic, and whether Turan's job was to reinforce public opinion or to shape it. "It must be awful to be

Kenneth Turan, to live in a world where, as near as I can figure, there hasn't been a halfway good film released since well before the original version of 'The Jazz Singer,'" wrote another reader. "Every Turan review reeks with the distaste he must feel, having to compare all of these sorry films to the utter masterpieces he would have made, if only he weren't too good for that sort of work."[111]

Turan's considered response to both irate readers and to Titanic's multiple Golden Globe wins[112] and Academy Award nominations was prescient – and its publication preceded the airing of the Oscar cere-mony itself on March 23, 1998. To a limited extent Titanic's budget served as a template for future filmmaking; Spider-Man 2 (2004) cost an outright $200 million, but it was the sequel of a proven blockbuster. More importantly, it was an indicator of future box office and audience expectations. And that, suggested Turan, would lead to more films with what he considered weak scripts and boilerplate plots, "which would likely solidify trends already apparent in Hollywood and lead, unless we're lucky, to changes in the kinds of movies we'll be seeing in the future, changes that all audiences will notice and not necessarily applaud."[113] It is certainly the case that the last few years have seen a precipitous drop in box office receipts. But he also took on the very specific criticism readers leveled at what his job was supposed to do for them. "General opinion notwithstanding," Turan suggested, film critics "are not intended to be applause meters. Just as restaurant critics don't send couples seeking that special anniversary meal straight to McDonald's on the 'everybody goes there, it must be the best' theory, the overall mandate of critics must be to point out the existence and importance of other criteria for judgment besides popularity."[114] An obvious point, it would seem, but one that appeared to need reiterating in the face of what Turan regarded as Titanic's "watershed" success. And this understanding of how important a mediocre (in Turan's opinion) film could be implicitly suggested that film critics, while not film his-torians, do well to take an historical view – something not incumbent on an audience. For Turan, Titanic's success was symptomatic of current conditions in Hollywood's industrial and corporate structure:

[W]hile Cameron's version is attracting paying customers in unprecedented numbers, that success paradoxically says at least as much
about how poor a job Hollywood in general is doing in reaching the
mass audience that should be its bread and butter as it does about
the filmmaking skill of its creators.

The flip side of "Titanic's" ability to draw hordes of viewers into
theaters is the question of where these viewers have been for the
past several years. In its unintentional underlining of how narrow an
audience net most movies cast, "Titanic" is not an example of
Hollywood's success, it's an emblem of its failure.

For "Titanic's" ability to attract a crowd also shows how desperate
the mainstream audience — alienated by studio reliance on the kind
of mindless violence that can be counted on to sell overseas — has
become for anything even resembling old-fashioned entertainment.[115]

Five days after *Titanic's* record-tying number of wins at the Academy
Awards, the *Los Angeles Times* published Cameron's retort on the front
page of its Calendar section. Cameron began by saying he could take
the *ad hominem* attacks month after month. But what had impelled him
to write, finally, was that Turan was "us[ing] his bully pulpit not only
to attack my film, but the entire film industry and its audiences."[116] The
newly anointed "King of the World" was defending his kingdom.

Again, what was really at stake (or seemed so on the debate's
face) was not a particular opinion of a particular film. Rather, it was
the critic's place in the fabric of film culture. For Cameron, Turan
had lost affection for films in general, and, worse – and as a consequence – had become fundamentally elitist, removed from the population he served:

Turan sees himself as the high priest of some arcane art form that is
far too refined for the average individual to possibly appreciate. He
writes as if the insensitive masses must be constantly corrected, like
little children who do not have the sense or experience to know what is
good for them without the critic's patient instruction. This is paternalism

and elitism in its worst form, and utterly insults the movie audience, which is theoretically his constituency.[117]

More generally, Cameron offered a decidedly populist estimation of the role of the film critic.

> When people spend their hard-earned money on a movie at the end of a long work week, all they ask is that their local critic steer them toward the good ones and help them avoid the turkeys. It's not too much to ask. And it's a fairly simple job, once you grasp it. You get to go to a movie first, before anyone else, and then come back and tell everybody about it. You even get to trash it if you didn't like it. What you don't get to do is grind on and on, month after month, after the audience has rendered its verdict in the most resounding of terms, telling everybody why the filmgoers are wrong and you are right.[118]

Cameron called for Turan's impeachment (a loaded word during the end of the Clinton years), and asked instead for a critic who "who respects the paying audiences who look to him or her for guidance, not for lectures on how stupid they are for liking what they like."[119] To be deliberately circular about it, this utterance was particularly symptomatic of Cameron's symptomatic nature. On the one hand, he defended the filmgoing public against elitist taste (simultaneously and probably unintentionally shoring up a distinction between high and low that many of the era's non-studio, independent films were breaking down); elsewhere in the response he reminded Turan that some significant portion of the audience had gone back for seconds and even thirds, implying that, though the critic might disagree with audience taste, there was no doubt that the public itself not only had an opinion, it had a strong one. On the other hand, he stressed the "paying" aspect of the audience, suggesting that the financial investment mattered as much as the emotional one, which he stressed heavily. Indeed, Cameron took the money expended on *Titanic* tickets to be a direct signifier of emotion. Citing the great number of countries around the world where the film was holding the top box office slot, he concluded, "audiences around the world are celebrating their own essential humanity by going into a dark room and crying together."[120] He did not allow that they could have been sharing anything else, certainly nothing less lofty. Just as telling, perhaps, was that Cameron had nothing to say about the sector of the audience who did not have a long workweek, or whose dollars were not hard earned, smaller though that sector surely was. That is: the spectator Cameron imagined for *Titanic* was far more like Jack and the other passengers in steerage than they were like Rose. A populist filmmaker imagining a popular audience for a popular film is nothing if not consistent, and one would hardly expect Cameron to make the kind of films that might appeal to Rose, a proto-feminist who collected avant-garde paintings. But what's so telling about Cameron's implicit equation is its clear suggestion that one of film's specific functions is to provide an escapism that is emotional in nature, suggesting Cameron's sense of everyday life under late consumer capitalism as devoid of precisely that collective emotionality that his film provides.

The debate between Cameron and Turan generated a meta-level when *Variety*, the Hollywood industry journal of record, chronicled not only the contretemps itself, but also the responses of other Hollywood insiders and film critics.[121] Critics, including Andrew Sarris of the *New York Observer*, Owen Gleiberman at *Entertainment Weekly*, Thelma Adams of the *New York Post*, and Frank Rich of the *New York Times* either concurred with Turan in his evaluation of *Titanic* or simply chided Cameron for his arrogance, both at the Academy Awards and in his letter to Turan. To be fair, if there were more modulated assertions in Cameron's letter, they remain unpublished. The *Los Angeles Times* cut it by one-third before running it boxed with his picture. Ultimately, following that letter, reader response ran 90 percent in favor of Turan.

POPULAR APPENDIX 2: POPOTLA VS. *TITANIC*

In spite of the serious issues at stake in the contretemps between Cameron and Turan, and the care each took to lay out their considered opinions and ideas, the debate could easily have been seen as so much hot air going back and forth between a well-established and influential critic and a well-established and influential filmmaker, neither of whom was in any danger of losing his job because of the quarrel. This is hardly to say that the conversation (including the voices of those who piped in from the sidelines) was meaningless, only that its implications were being worked out in relatively hypothetical ways at that point – realities of the box office notwithstanding. Real and concrete fallout from the making of *Titanic* had already occurred on Rosarito Beach in Popotla, Mexico, where Cameron had built his 90 percent scale model of the ship, as well as a 17 million gallon tank to hold it. While the tank and its attendant soundstage continue to be used by Fox Studios, the local residents still question the benefits of this new industry in their hometown. A security wall six feet high and 500 feet long was built around the studio, the result of which was that the indigenous fishing community no longer had access to the ocean. It would have made little difference had access existed, as the sea urchins, a major fishing crop, had been damaged by the chlorinated water spilling out of the studio's tank into the Pacific Ocean. At the Popotla community's request, two United States artists, James Bleisner and Luz Camacho, formed RevocionArte, which helped the residents construct an ongoing artwork on the exterior walls of the Rosarito studio. This was a low-tech effort both to critique the high-tech, corporate conditions that had disenfranchised the Popotlans from their own livelihood, and to beautify what was an enormous eyesore. The project used found objects like rusty bedsprings and beer cans to create a three-dimensional mural that represented exactly what they had lost with the arrival of this Hollywood *maquiladora*. The irony of this low-tech intervention against what was state of the art movie-making was apparent to many, and Ars Electronica, the Austrian digital culture foundation, gave awards to both Digital Domain (Cameron's special effects company) for its advanced computer animation and also to RevocionArte and Popotla for the wall, what Ars Electronica's artistic director Gerfried Stocker called "a symbol for available low-tech against expensive high-tech."[122]

FISHING VILLAGE WINS PRIZE FOR TECHNOLOGICAL WARFARE (Ars Electronica "Infoweapon Award" press release August 4, 1998)

Ars Electronica, the foremost new media technology festival in the world, has awarded its prestigious InfoWeapon cash prize to the people of Popotla, a tiny Mexican fishing village, for resisting unwanted technologies by means of trash and recycled materials.

To film the movie *Titanic*, Twentieth Century Fox built a sort of "movie maquiladora" in Popotla, and surrounded it with a giant cement wall to keep the villagers out. ("Maquiladora" is the term for U.S. factories operating in Mexico because of the low wages.) The people of Popotla reacted to the unsightly wall first in humiliation and anger, and then by covering it with a mural constructed from garbage they amassed and collected. The Ars Electronica InfoWeapon jury is rewarding Popotla for this remarkable low-tech gesture against an unpleasant high-tech situation.

Ars Electronica is also awarding the movie *Titanic* itself, which cost US$200 million to make, its Golden Nica cash prize for computer animation. Ars Electronica is thus in the cutting-edge position of rewarding both parties in a cultural and economic dispute that some consider unresolvable.[123]

Ars Electronica may have been on the cutting edge of awards, but in some sense the organization had simply awarded the two groups to a draw. Even the cash awards were lopsided: $10,000 to Digital Domain, $1,000 to the Popotlans. Some felt the allocation should have been reversed. "You gave both the corporate hogs and their victims some cash?" opined one participant on an Ars Electronica mailing list. "Big fucking whoop."[124] Big fucking whoop, indeed. The Digital Domain award recipient, Robert Legato, apparently was completely unaware of the Popotla mural.

The Popotlan community cannily mobilized a pair of artists to help them engage in creative protest. It was a protest that, though representational in nature, was also conceptual, as the specific images were constructed out of trash (how the Popotlans felt *Titanic* was treating them). The piece had two audiences: the Popotlans, for whom it was both a project of social critique and neighborhood beautification, and the wider world, for whom, accessible largely by images, it would be seen strictly as the former. Few were likely to visit Popotla, so the entire chain of events, as the community well knew, would only be articulated through the media, and was likely to be understood only if framed by one of the agents of its creation. Fernando Larios Zepeda, spokesperson for the Popotla Fishermen's Association issued this statement:

Popotla Fishermen's Statement, September 12, 1998

[Popotlans] have been there for many years, living from the sea ... they do not abuse their ecology, they take only what they need ... Just in front ... was one of the most beautiful underwater gardens; with enormous kelp beds ... home to million[s of] living creatures ... abalone, sea urchin, lobster and many kinds of valuable fish; this garden is famous world wide, among the scuba divers, because of its beauty and fullness of underwater life ...

These humble, but proud people, pay their taxes ... live on their own private land ... employ a lot of Mexican people ... do not want any economic help from their government ... do not try to cross the border with the United States ... they ... live well the way they are, they just want to be left alone ...

In only a few weeks, the movie studios were built, they did not gave [sic] job[s] to anybody from the little town, they erected very tall walls [with] armed guards on top of them ... The fishermen were left powerless ...

In The Studios [sic] construction, they used explosives underwater, destroying life kilometers around ... they built a giant water pool to film the Titanic; they filled [it] with millions of liters of sea water; and ...

they added a lot of chlorine, when they were true [sic] filming a scene, they emptied the tank directly into the Pacific Ocean ... the fishermen, with the press as witness, took the samples and sent them to private but faithful laboratories; they found the chlorine, solvents and human waste in very high concentrations; even with those proofs, the authorities did not want to listen ...

To protest the tall walls, they permitted and helped a group of international artist to decorate those ugly walls, that now, blocked the ocean view; and, a work of art was created ...

[S]ince the studios operate, the production of sea urchin have drooped [sic] from 10 tons a year to 6 and then to almost none; most of the valuable fishes, have emigrated, because of the chlorine and noise; what use [sic] to be a beautiful underwater jungle is almost dead; where they use to have a beautiful ocean view, there is only the beauty created by the artists on the walls ...

We only hope, that Mexican law will be respected, that money dirty from destruction of the ecology will not be able to buy justice, and, that prosperity can go hand in hand with equality for everybody.

The ecology is not a Mexican issue, it is a global problem, and, art, is the true international language.[125]

If art is an international language, culturally specific though any utterance of it may be, then *Titanic* is certainly one of its most legible articulations. But its legibility, as that of all Cameron films, is unstable, constantly shifting, and as the broad variety of analyses by these many scholars and critics has shown, subject to debate.

3

THE EYE OF CAMERON'S CAMERA:

Cinema as Reflexive Vision Machine

The cinema of James Cameron has always had a heightened relationship to vision, one that far exceeds its status as cinema. Cameron is not
interested simply in showing something cinematically, spectacularly or
otherwise. Rather, all of his films have repeated moments that, to vary-
ing degrees of subtlety and reflexivity, remind the spectator that the
narrative in question is being presented to them by a vision machine –
the camera and the attendant post-production special effects. However
much any viewer may be drawn into a Cameron film, emotionally or
viscerally, Cameron narratives tend to present their credentials as films,
as something made by someone to be seen by someone, at some point in the course
of the diegesis. These moments, resonant and significant though they
often are, never override the dominant mode of Cameron's work,
which is one of absorption and straightforward entertainment.
Nevertheless, without these moments, some of them the most intricate
and meaningful in his films, we might not read the more direct majority of his narrative aesthetic in quite the same ways. Far from being
instances of empty reflexivity, exercises in the self-referential for their
own sake, these sequences activate a discourse of the meta-cinematic,
inciting the spectator to take a more active investment in the film as a

spectator. Interestingly, this activation need not be socio-political, but can be purely structural. That is, rather than inevitably promoting an awareness of what it might mean at any given place and time to be a spectator of a big budget spectacle (though they very well may), these moments intensify the spectator's experience of the film at the level of the act of seeing itself.

THE TERMINATOR (1984)

Cameron signals his preoccupation with vision and its relation to identity early on in his work. Thirty-seven minutes into his first major feature film, Cameron elaborates on the unique capacities of the Terminator and how he sees the world. Having already established his strength, mechanical nature, and ability to deduce his way (via the execution of two other Sarah Connors) to the correct Sarah Connor, Cameron presents us with a literalized view of the Terminator's vision. As he chases Sarah and Kyle Reese down an alley, we see his point of view. If every other aspect of his "character" could so far still be human, even if homicidal, psychopathic, or otherwise extreme, his vision is the definitive articulation of his machine nature. It is an infrared screen that combines a number of different readings and readouts: a compass, a target sight centered on Sarah and Reese, and a variety of data, program directives, and codes that move so fast the spectator can't possibly read them – though, as a cyborg, of course, the Terminator can. The machine eye computes the world in terms of very particular information that is mathematical, weapons related, and task and goal oriented. Significantly, Cameron does not introduce this vital element until just after Sarah and Reese have met and have at least provisionally made an alliance. The two humans have begun their courtship of survival, at which point Cameron confirms what will in this film be held as the human's opposite. (This binary changes, of course, in Terminator 2.) It is not without interest that, in a subsequent flashback – or flashforward, depending on how one structures the relation between story and discourse in the film – Reese's point of view when looking through the night-sight of a firearm in his own present time is also a field of data readouts. But these readouts come far closer to having a syntax that makes them legible to the spectator, suggesting the difference between *using* technology and *being* technology. Cameron proposes that the technology is capable of learning the syntax, and subsequent points of view become more legible to the spectator, and less a jumble of meaningless (to us) numbers. The next time we see the infrared vision, the Terminator uses it to choose from a short list of possible responses to a janitor outside his flophouse door. Scrolling down the list, he stops at "Fuck you, asshole." It works, and the custodian leaves him alone and moves on. Not only is this a humorous moment, it is also an efficient primer about filmmaking. The actor playing the Terminator has read a script, and once on set reads lines for the camera that will seem like unrehearsed dialog to the viewer. This is exactly what the Terminator does in the diegesis.

In a scene about 51 minutes into *The Terminator*, the Terminator repairs his own body parts, which have been damaged during a high-speed chase with Sarah, Reese and the L.A. Police. The repairs are intercut with Reese being interrogated by Dr. Silberman (Earl Boen), a police psychiatrist, who is trying to determine whether Reese is crazy (by this time the audience is quite certain he is not). Reese is observed by the psychiatrist, but he can also see himself in a two-way mirror, an image that reflects back to him his drama in a way that approximates what the spectator sees – he is both agent and audience of his narrative. Behind the glass are Lieutenant Traxler (Paul Winfield) and Detective Vucovich (Lance Henriksen), who observe Reese and Dr. Silberman unseen. But, multiplying technologies of the visible even further, these two men watch the interrogation take place while a live video feed of the same scene plays on a monitor behind them. (When they approach the mirror, their images are also doubled in the glass, often making the frame seem more crowded than it really is.) No one observes this monitor except the spectator – and the film camera positioned to show it to us, an image apparatus gazing on an image apparatus. In this case, the doubled apparatic vision reinforces for the spectator the truth of Reese's sanity, because we see images that the psychiatrist and police officers do not. In its privileged relation to the spectator, it is even possible to regard Reese's video image – an external representation displaced not only from Reese but to another room altogether – as a visual representation of his unconscious, or his inner self, something in which the yawning, beeper-checking psychiatrist is not in fact all that interested. Cameron also delivers psychological interiority and depth in a far more traditional way. In a scene largely constructed of two-shots and over-the-shoulder two-shots, Reese is the only character allowed to occupy the frame on his own, as he intensely describes that he cannot return to the future, his own present tense, and battle the Terminator on his own. Alone in the image, he explains, "It's just him . . . and me."

What the Terminator's vision tells us might be another matter. There is no question as to his interiority – he has none. It is not until the self-repair scene that the spectator becomes quite certain of that. Nevertheless, the sequence implies that he has been given some kind of mechanical replacement for subjectivity, though hardly an equivalent, and as Cameron moves the camera around, providing close-ups, extreme close-ups and reestablishing shots, we are presented with the Terminator, his reflection, and the occasional objective angle. This produces a curious kind of self-regard in the cyborg. In order to do the repairs, the Terminator must look at himself in the mirror of his flophouse room to fix an eye that has become damaged in the previous firefight. The flesh is beyond repair, and, gazing intently on its reflection, the Terminator takes an Exacto knife and cuts it away, revealing it to be as unnecessary as the spectator has come to suspect. As he wipes off the remaining blood and bits of flesh, we are presented with the mechanical eye – the eye that has been doing the looking all along. It does not need the humanoid flesh to see; it merely needs it to blend in with actual humans. Now that the mechanical eye is exposed (which would expose the Terminator for what he really is), the solution is to replace physical camouflage with fashion. Before he exits his hotel room, the Terminator puts on a pair of wraparound sunglasses.

FIGURE 3.1 The now iconic figure of the Terminator.
Orion / The Kobal collection

The viewer has already seen the infrared Terminator vision from the cyborg's point of view in earlier sequences. So, although that technology is not shown in this scene, the spectator fills in that highly personalized (though highly impersonal) field whenever a point of view shot of the Terminator is shown. There are two key details to note here: first, the Terminator removes his irreparably damaged organic eye by slicing through it in precisely the way a woman's eye is famously bisected in Luis Buñuel and Salvador Dali's surrealist classic Un Chien Andalou (1928), though in that film the complete slicing is implied first in a thin line of clouds passing like a knife over a full moon, and then in the actual cutting of a dead animal's eye that is clearly not the woman's. Here, though, the slicing is self-inflicted, though at no painful cost.

Second, once the organic material has been removed, and unceremoniously (and painlessly) dropped in the sink, Cameron lingers on a close-up of the mechanical eye, which looks like, functions like, is a camera lens, its iris rotating open and shut. (For some this will recall nothing so much as Dziga Vertov's The Man with a Movie Camera (1929).) The film camera looks at the cyber-camera, and the audience looks at the one through the other. This is merely the most apparent in a series of moments in all of Cameron's films that are reflexive gestures to the act of seeing – though what each one of them means is, of course, specific to the film-text it inhabits. Given Cameron's establishment in The Terminator of what critics have called a "tech-noir" aesthetic (named after the nightclub in the film), a set of visual codes that uses technology to point toward technology's dystopian functions, this particular instance of the spectator's organic eye looking at a mechanical reflection of itself might offer up new ways to think about technology's implications for the postmodern subject.

ALIENS (1986)

The Terminator presented the Oedipal quandary of John Connor choosing his own father and then sending him back in time to save – and have procreative sex with – his mother. The theatrical release of Aliens, trimmed for length, gives no hint of these issues, but in the director's cut Cameron returns to a similar wet knot, and depicts it in typical meta-representational ways. Early in this version, just before Ripley (Sigourney Weaver) is to go into a hearing about what happened on the *Nostromo* (the events represented in *Alien*), she is told that, having been in hypersleep for 57 years, her daughter (who is not mentioned in either the first *Alien* or the theatrical release of the sequel) has died at the age of 66, two years before Ripley's rescue. A photograph of her daughter shows a smiling, grey-haired, wrinkled woman old enough to be Ripley's mother. Ripley's daughter married, but, unlike Ripley, never had children, her mother's unexplained disappearance tacitly standing as her motive. (Then again, the smile on her face doesn't suggest she was entirely traumatized by her mother's unexplained absence.) This produces a discourse in which Ripley is younger than her dead daughter, and also creates a framework of maternal guilt – "I promised her I'd be home for her birthday . . . her eleventh birthday" – which explains her subsequent attachment to Newt on the terra-forming colony. Ripley strokes the photograph – a

FIGURE 3.2 Newt provides Ripley with a chance for redemptive motherhood.
20th Century Fox / The Kobal collection

representation standing in indexically for the absent person (an absence never again to be a presence), kisses it, and weeps for her loss. This photograph holds an importance for Ripley similar to the photograph Reese carries with him of Sarah – a representation not only of a person and a love object with whom some kind of union or reunion is intensely desired, but also a representation of the complexities (even impossibilities) of the space–time givens of the narrative – complexities cinema is particularly qualified both to represent and to smooth out.

This shot of Ripley with her daughter's image is immediately followed by another shot that also presents the viewer with photographs of dead people (the crew of the *Nostromo*). Like the photograph of Ripley's daughter, they are accompanied by text with basic data, serving as a visual match, and equating the two sets of images, tracing the magnitude of Ripley's losses, personal and professional. One by one, images of the crew of the *Nostromo* flash behind Ripley on a large screen as she testifies to the Company board about what happened in *Alien* (just in case anyone in the audience has not seen the first film). Finally, just as Ripley is told that she is having her pilot's license suspended, her own image comes up on the screen behind her. Without her professional identity, she might as well be dead.

But Ripley's professional identity hinged on an old model of corporate capitalism, one in which the governmental and the corporate spheres were separate. When Earth loses contact with LV-426, the site of the original alien encounter and in the sequel a terraforming colony co-financed by "The Company" and the "Colonial Administration," company lackey Carter Burke (Paul Reiser) comes to Ripley for help. That the actants in this drama are all clearly American, but that the (not too distant) future is framed not in terms of national identities and boundaries but in terms of colonies and corporations – whose boundaries are themselves significantly blurred – seems symptomatic of the film's production during the Reagan years. Deregulation resulted in the rise of corporate influence so exponentially expanded that it often seemed to supplant national(ist) influence.[1] Here, a reluctant Ripley is asked to accompany the Colonial Marines as an "adviser," certainly echoing the presence of military advisers in Nicaragua, Honduras, and elsewhere under Reagan. It is not without import that Burke does not say the United States Marines. Even though later the Marines' uniforms bear a U.S. flag, and a label that says "U.S.C.M." (not United States Marine Corp but United States Colonial Marines), the country is never named, as if to say that in the early twenty-first century, the corporate has indeed superseded the national in power and importance, or at least been conflated with it. The various slogans that adorn the Marines' clothing, uniforms, and firearms bear this out: one wears a T-shirt that says "Peace through Super Firepower," making transparent what the Reagan-era slogan "Peace through Strength" really meant. A military pilot has written the United Airlines commercial tagline "Fly the Friendly Skies" on her helmet.

As in The Terminator, Cameron seldom goes for long without presenting some form of mediated vision. Ripley's decision to accompany the Marines occurs during a scene where she talks to Burke not directly but on videophone, so that she speaks to his image, even if it is a live transmission. In the following scene, our first introduction to the Marine company is not by way of their images, but through a computer screen that lists their names and relevant data, a screen that evokes not only the earlier sequence in the film that logged the Nostromo crew, but also the Terminator's field of vision in Cameron's previous feature. The computer screen, filling with text, dissolves to a shot of the Marines, Burke, the android Bishop (Lance Henriksen), and Ripley in hypersleep.

Cameron maintains this doubly framed mode of vision throughout Aliens. In an extended sequence, the Marines search for surviving colonists in the Atmosphere Processor of the terraforming colony. Ripley, Lieutenant Gorman (William Hope) and Company man Burke all observe from the safety of the Armored Personnel Carrier (APC). Their view is enabled by the views of the video cameras affixed to the Marines' helmets. A "preview" of the technology has been shown to the audience during the drop to the surface of LV-426, and the initial sweep of the living quarters, when events are not chaotic. That we will rely on this technology to make sense of things is signaled to us by

Lieutenant Gorman who, as he scans the banks of video monitors, says as much to himself as to anyone else, "All right . . . let's see what we can see." As the commanding officer, he directs the soldiers just as Cameron directs his actors. "Drake," he says to one private, "check your camera. There seems to be a malfunction." Drake (Mark Rolston) fixes the problem the old fashioned, low-tech way – by banging his head and the camera attached to it against a hard surface, like someone banging the side of a pre-cable television set to clear up the reception. Gorman further instructs Drake in specifically cinematic terms, "Pan it around a bit . . . good." Only the pilot observes the landscape of LV-426 with an unmediated visual. Everyone else sees its video representation before venturing outside.

Even when they leave the drop ship, the soldiers themselves take in the new and potentially dangerous landscape not purely by human sight, but continue to rely on the information on the video monitors – as relayed to them by Gorman – to know what the rest of the squad is doing elsewhere in the colony. Ripley and the others in the APC can

FIGURE 3.3 The Marines rely on technologies of vision as much as the spectator does.
20th Century Fox / The Kobal collection

only survey the area through technologically mediated (mediatized) vision. But even the men and women on the scene who are "really" there look to "video-aiming monitors" and "motion trackers" to tell them what they are looking at. Those in the APC – and the audience – see far more than what the Marines see. Also visible on the readout monitors are the vital signs of each soldier. As some sustain mortal injury after encountering the aliens, those readings flatline, and the camera, once a sign for the vision of a living person, returns to its purely automated state, no longer subjective, no longer a stand-in for the view of a human being. With their automated vision and accompanying data readouts, the Marines are provisionally rendered cyborg. And while the audience sharing the Terminator's vision puts it in a privileged position not shared by the other characters in The Terminator and T2, in Aliens the enhanced field of view is accessible to both the spectator and all of the characters. What distinguishes the Marines from the Terminator is, of course, their physical fallibility – the fact that, unlike the Terminator, they can be killed, and die in pain, puts definitive limits on those claims.[2]

Cameron achieves something remarkable in these sequences. Layering technologies of the visual one atop another is a transparent acknowledgement that the images in front of the viewer are made, created, not happening naturally. And yet, the layering actually has the almost paradoxical effect of bringing spectators even closer to the action (or at least feeling that they are). If viewers have no choice but to rely on Cameron's camera to present the events at hand, they are in a position no different from the actants in the diegesis, who also rely on similar technologies to inform them. Ripley, who knows more than the other characters, can only watch the monitors helplessly as events take a deadly turn. The spectator, having seen the original Alien, also knows more than the other characters, and this status of "knowing more" along with Ripley further enhances audience identification with her. Having bought a ticket to a film that is likely to offer the same violent thrills as The Terminator, the spectator is put in the position of identifying with the single character in the film who wants no part of that violence – even if, in the end, Ripley will be the ultimate purveyor of that violence. In the first reconnaissance sequence, Cameron further aligns us with Ripley by aligning her with both Corporal Hicks (Michael Biehn) and himself. As often as not, Ripley receives information from the Marines through Hicks's camera, and that vision brings the two of them into an intimate relationship borne out later in the film (see my Introduction).[3] Later on, Hicks will give Ripley what looks like a wrist-watch but is in fact a locator, so he can find her no matter where she is, very much like the motion sensors that tell the Marines where the aliens are. The scene is shot in tightly framed medium-close-up two shots, and when Ripley thanks Hicks, he wryly responds, "it doesn't mean we're engaged or anything." Yet in the overall logic of the film, it might as well, especially since Ripley subsequently puts the locator on Newt, thus completing a kind of familial circuit that will become far more explicit by the end of the film.[4]

As Hicks moves through the reconnaissance mission, Ripley directs him just as Gorman had earlier directed Drake – and Hicks is the only Marine she coaches in this way. Spotting something in his field of vision whose meaning he cannot possibly understand, but which Ripley knows all too well (tell-tale signs of alien acid blood eating through the floors), she says, "Hicks, back up. Pan right."[5] Hicks now functions not as a human being with interpretive capacities but simply as a camera eye, concerned mostly that Ripley is "seeing this OK." Together, Hicks (the visual technology) and Ripley (the comprehend-ing brain) make up one subject, whose hybrid nature relates to both that of the Terminator and that of the "synthetic human," Bishop, how-ever temporarily.

This equation of human vision with mechanical vision, and its re-equation with the vision of the film spectator is frankly proposed even in the packaging of *Aliens* for home entertainment. The entry panels for the special edition DVD of *Aliens* (in which Cameron restored 17 minutes of footage 20th Century Fox required him to cut – including the dis-closure that Ripley had a daughter on Earth) are recreations of the transmissions via helmet camera of the Marines, and every new panel represents the vision of a different Marine. For the spectator, as for Ripley *et al.*, viewing the film from a safe remove means investing in the visual capacities of those who are right in the action, whether they are the Marines or James Cameron himself. Indeed, the menu panel makes even more explicit the equation of shooting a film and shooting a firearm that military films inevitably produce, implicitly raising Cameron, the director, to the level of a general, and, as a consequence, militarizing the act of Hollywood filmmaking (see Paul Virilio, p. 62–65 in Chapter 2).[6] This militarization dovetails so easily with the building of the family that resolves the narrative, and has something to do with Cameron's stated intentions about how he specifically wanted his sequel to differ from the original. If the 17 restored minutes make explicit a storyline of maternal guilt and redemption, the film's deliberate relation to Vietnam is something Cameron confirmed in interviews. Looking for reasons that Ripley would go back into a dangerous situation when she does not have to, Cameron gives her both the grief and guilt over the absence from and loss of her daughter, and also a particular kind of attachment to the scene of danger. "When you come that close to death, whether it's a car accident or you're in combat," suggested Cameron, "you tend to fixate on that moment in your life . . . and what showed up in Vietnam was that people who were there for over a year would go back – even though it was the worst thing that ever happened to them."[7] Though in every other respect Ripley stands apart from the Marines as decidedly non-military (and stands equally apart from Burke as decidedly non-corporate), she suffers from trauma not unlike some returning war veterans.

THE ABYSS (1989)

Though still profitable, *The Abyss* was Cameron's least successful film, going over budget and long on its shooting schedule. These overruns largely stemmed from the exponentially more complicated circumstances of filming so much of the story underwater. The result, however, is a film that manages to imbue water with the same infinite dimensions and possibilities as space – and it is the single film that

FIGURE 3.4 Kubrick's film *2001: A Space Odyssey* made Cameron want to be a director.

MGM / The Kobal collection

most bears out Cameron's assertion that it was Stanley Kubrick's *2001:A Space Odyssey* (1968) that made him want to be a director. That the action now takes place neither on land nor in space, as had Cameron's previous films, but in the water, does not change Cameron's investment in multilayered visual technologies. Indeed, about midway through the theatrical release version of *The Abyss* (considerably shorter than the director's cut, which clocked in at 171 minutes), Cameron chooses to use several different kinds of mediating visual technology in consecutive sequences, such that the spectator never goes very long without having to negotiate such intervention.

Rig designer Lindsey (Mary Elizabeth Mastrantonio), her estranged husband Bud (Ed Harris), and Bud's crew discover that, against orders, and mistaking an unidentified alien presence for a Soviet nuclear sub, Navy SEAL Lieutenant Coffey (Michael Biehn) has smuggled a nuclear warhead onto their oilrig from a sunken American nuclear sub the SEALs had been sent down to rescue. Lindsey and Hippy (Todd Graff) conspire to use "Big Geek," a small camera submersible, to document the non-terrestrial intelligence (NTI), thereby proving that there is no Soviet threat, and thus convince Coffey that his warhead is unnecessary. The submersible is comically painted to look like a World War II fighter plane, with a mouth full of teeth, and the camera lens is clearly visible where its eyes would be. Between its face and its name, it is technology that is, if not anthropomorphized, certainly animalized, and though it doesn't have superhuman (or homicidal) capabilities, it is possible to consider it in the same category as the Terminator, whose mechanical eye is understood to be the closest thing it has to subjectivity. This is borne out later when Hippy talks to it as if it were sentient.

The scene opens with a 25-second long take starting with a close-up of Lindsey, but it is really a close-up of the video monitor with Lindsey's face filling its frame (a frame within a frame) that gives us Big Geek's point-of-view, complete with data readings including compass, depth, and more – *The Terminator* and *Aliens* redux. The camera dollies right to reveal the "real" Lindsey, much like Cameron's camera moves between a video image of Sarah Connor and the "real" Sarah Connor in a crucial scene in T2 (see below). In this case, the reflexivity of vision is further intensified. Where Sarah has no control over her video image (or any other, for that matter), here the dolly shows us that Lindsey herself is controlling Big Geek's camera, and looking straight into the lens. She is not only the image but its author as well – though Cameron of course remains the ultimate author. (As it happens, though, the way the apparatus is set up prevents Lindsey from authoring her image and seeing it at the same time, so she can never really be certain of the outcome of her control.) Moreover, Lindsey and Hippy are debating an act of vision itself – whether it is prudent or not to send Big Geek to document – that is, *to see and to make images of* – the alien life form in order to prove to the renegade SEALs that the foreign presence is not a Soviet nuclear submarine. The completed arc (very similar to the camera movement in Sarah's therapy session in T2, see below) stops so that Lindsey and Hippy are in a two-shot (a three-shot if we include Big Geek), with yet more video monitors showing their images in the background, slightly out of focus.

This shot is followed by a re-framed, high-angle two-shot (seven seconds in duration) of Lindsey and Hippy, but this one is radically different. It is the point-of-view of a surveillance camera, grainy and black and white. The sound quality has changed too, and is now muffled to reflect the generally diminished clarity of the image. Cameron offers the spectator less, not more, but this reduction opens up a question: if this is a surveillance image, who is watching? That question is answered in the next shot, which shows Coffey observing what Lindsey and Hippy believe is a private conversation, on the upper-left and clearest of five closed-circuit monitors. There is a return to the original surveillance shot, and then a cut to a tense Coffey digesting the new facts. Through these visuals Cameron articulates a complex and tense balance of information. On the one hand, Lindsey and Hippy know what Coffey does not – that these are NTIs, not Soviets. On the other, Coffey knows what Lindsey and Hippy do not – that their gathering of images through Big Geek will not be a secret between Lindsey and Hippy at all.

This triangulated scene among Lindsey, Hippy, and Coffey is followed by one in which surveillance and other screen technologies yet again play a crucial role. Most of the crew is asleep in the mess hall and sonar shack, including Sonny (J.C. Quinn) whose job it is to monitor the sonar and other systems seen behind him on a bank of screens while he snores with his back to them. As the camera tracks in to Sonny, it is only the spectator who can read the monitors going haywire behind him, a sure sign of what the following shot confirms – the alien life form is in the vicinity of the rig. Taking the form of a gentle, moving column of sea water, the alien being comes into the rig, and we see things from its point-of-view: undulating, as if we are also in, or under, water. Significantly, the first object the alien sets its gaze on is Big Geek – whose job it is to document the very form that now regards it. But Big Geek is "asleep," and so sees nothing. The column of water makes its way to the mess hall, and Lindsey is the first encounter it. As the rest of the crew wake up around her, the column of water presents itself to Lindsey as a liquid image of her own face, reminding us of her doubled image in the previous scene. It then transforms into Bud's face.

That the column of water can screen back to any character their own image is not the only way Cameron renders this manifestation of the NTI as a quasi-cinematic entity – or, put another way, finds a narrative

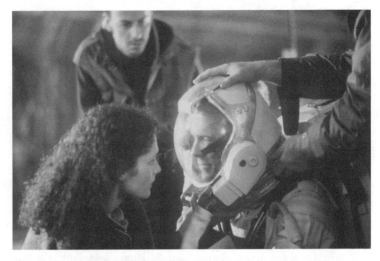

FIGURE 3.5 Lindsey's reconciliation with Bud requires her to resume certain traditional gender roles.
20th Century Fox / The Kobal collection / Foreman, Richard

rationale to turn water into something like a film screen. Towards the end of the film, Bud has successfully descended into the titular abyss and dismantled the rogue nuclear warhead, preventing it from detonating and starting World War Three. Because he is breathing liquid oxygen, and can't speak, his communication with Lindsey and the others has been via a type pad affixed to his wrist. As a result, his speech is rendered text, that is to say image, and that text/image is legible on one of the many monitors with which the audience has become familiar in the course of the narrative. After defusing the warhead, Bud finds he doesn't have enough oxygen to return to the surface. He types his farewell, as seen on the monitor, "KNEW THIS WAS ONE-WAY TICKET. BUT YOU KNOW I HAD TO COME." This is followed by the reconciliation between Bud and Lindsey. His final typed words to her are, "LOVE YOU. WIFE." In Bud's hailing of Lindsey as wife, she is not only reconciled with her husband (though, as will also be the case in *Titanic*, at the cost of the male partner's life – in this case only apparent), she is also rehabilitated from her position as "bitch," the word most commonly used to describe her throughout the film, and one that she takes on herself. (Indeed, it is only when she takes it on herself, as she talks Bud down through the Abyss, that the film sees her as having sufficiently internalized traditional gender norms to be once again worthy of Bud.)

As Bud waits to die, he is rescued by one of the non-terrestrial intelligent life forms and taken to the underwater city. As he enters, light is reflected off his visor in a way that not only directly refers to 2001, but also provides yet another screen on which images play, pointing to the visuality of the film yet again.[8] Bud cannot survive in the underwater world of the NTIs without help, so they make an air chamber for him with walls of seawater. These walls not only enclose breathable air, they are also transformed into a movie screen that does for Bud, when speaking to the NTIs (who do not, in fact, talk back, or speak at all), the very same thing that his type pad did for him while dismantling the warhead. Just as the NTIs offered Lindsey and Bud visual representations of themselves as a way of communicating, so the NTIs now explain their rationale for saving Bud – his sacrificial act and his love for his wife – by showing him his own typed words ("Knew this was one-way ticket . . . ") on a new screen, effectively making Bud not only the enunciator of his words but also the receiver, and, quite visibly, the spectator of them. In the director's cut this scene is significantly extended (by four minutes) and produces a protracted and further complicated spectatorial position for Bud. Explaining to Bud their presence on Earth, they show him television news broadcasts describing the heating up of the Cold War, as well as reports of tsunami-like "acoustical shockwaves" spreading the world over. The NTIs are poised to destroy the world with a flood of biblical proportions, and Bud asks them why they would do so. In response they screen images of the twentieth-century history of Extremely Bad Human Behavior, from the Holocaust to the detonation of nuclear bombs to Vietnam and beyond on the makeshift sea wall. Bud watches all of this, well-informed, but helpless to do anything about it (not unlike Ripley in *Aliens*), not only because he is 20,000 leagues under the sea, but also because what the

NTIs are screening for him is history. Eventually the NTIs pull the walls of water back from the world's coastlines, restoring safety and, slightly inexplicably – since no one besides Bud knows what caused the tsunamis in the first place – allowing the peoples of the world to conclude peace is better than war in so doing. In this scene, their rationale for saving the world (and not just Bud) is Bud's selfless, loving actions. Bud observes all of this on the water screens, as does the audience. In this version, Cameron's progressive critique of the Cold War (which is not as explicit in the theatrical release) is rendered more conservative than it might be, since the NTI's inspiration to save the world (from itself and from them) turns on the romantic sacrifices of one heroic white male and his restored hetero-normative marriage.

TERMINATOR 2: JUDGMENT DAY (1991)

Developments in special effects, many of them Cameron's own, made the visual images in Terminator 2 resemble far more what Cameron would have liked in the original film. The innovations are signaled almost immediately (within the film's first six minutes) by the familiar infrared view of Schwarzenegger's Terminator's vision. Now, however, it is less blurry, more legible, and there is a variety of textual information now available to the spectator that was not there in the first film. This information functions almost as the Terminator's interior monologue, sorting out his priorities for the spectator in the absence of emotional expressions on his face. It is also a way to fill in the Terminator's terse dialog, as in an early scene when the cyborg, just having traveled across time, walks into a biker bar stark naked. He scans the room to find a customer whose clothing will fit him, and this is presented to the spectator as an infrared version of the "regular" frame. The T101 sees a promising figure (the data tells him – and us – so), and the cigar smoking biker's body is outlined on the screen. Our vision is aligned with that of the Terminator, if only briefly. This time, because the Terminator is a "good guy," this is both more comfortable, and, in terms of screen time, a more sustained strategy by Cameron.

However, not all of the striking visual effects in T2 were new developments. Indeed, some were resonant particularly in their retrograde nature – retrogressions that explicitly referred to the original film. Sarah Connor, now incarcerated in a hospital for the criminally insane, is overseen by Dr. Silberman (Earl Boen), the same police psychiatrist who evaluated Kyle Reese's sanity in The Terminator. In the sequel, Sarah is interviewed by Dr. Silberman, just as Kyle was. But rather than having a live video feed, in Terminator 2, she and Silberman watch, and "critique," a previous therapy session, in which she describes her repeated nightmares of nuclear Armageddon. By the end of the scene, with the promise of a visit with her son, Dr. Silberman has convinced her to disavow her Cassandra-like warning of nuclear war – though she clearly privately still believes it.

The script describes the doubled effect of Sarah watching her own image, and the implications of the spectator watching both are clear.[9] What Cameron does in the actual shooting, however, is even more complex and multivalent. First, the video interview that Sarah and the doctor watch is not shown to us as having been shot by a fixed camera – the positioning that would be par for the course for institutional documentation. Rather, it periodically zooms in on Sarah for emphasis, providing in a single take what Cameron could not achieve with cutting on the monitor to a close up, as that would have detracted from the verisimilitude of the surveillance, and consequently the realism of the scene. Second, after Dr. Silberman pauses the videotape, Sarah sits down across the table from him. Cameron dollies around in an arc (just as he does in the "Big Geek" scene in The Abyss described above), and stops only when the "real Sarah" and Dr. Silberman are in the foreground, and when one wall of the room has revealed itself to be a mirror, on which the audience can see not only the reflection of the real Sarah and Dr. Silberman, but the reflection of Sarah's video image on the monitor as well – an image of an image of an image. When the camera does pull back from the interview room (in the editing process this comes a few lines later than it does in the final script), it reveals in the adjacent room not only the interns and psychologists mentioned in the screenplay, but also a man operating a video camera and a back of monitors as well. The camera finally comes to rest on a live feed of the current interview, a close up on Sarah's face. If in *The Terminator*, the multiple images functioned to confirm Kyle's sanity in the face of contemporary and authoritarian institutions that did not believe him (institutions in the form of their human representatives), here the layering is more equivocal. The audience does not doubt the existence of the Terminator, but the substance of the session is the recounting of Sarah's recurring dream. Dreams are a kind of cinema of the unconscious, and that Sarah's recurs suggests the infinitely re-playable quality of a movie as well. Moreover, though the spectator does not doubt that Sarah is likely to be right, unlike the Terminator, she has no real proof of the nuclear disaster. That is, in the context of a movie that represents an enormous and expensive fiction, one requiring a *very* willing suspension of disbelief (though no more than any other science fiction film), the dream, as a less reliable visual narrative, makes the film itself more reliable, and, as a consequence, provisionally puts Sarah's complete sanity into some doubt, all of which will play in to how the spectator reads her as a mother later on in the film (see Chapter 2).

TRUE LIES (1994)

If Cameron's previous films had been action and science fiction hybrids that also contained comedic elements, *True Lies* was the first film he wrote and directed intentionally designed to foreground comedy and use action to do it. This was a relatively easy mix to achieve given his choice of Arnold Schwarzenegger to star in what would be their third collaboration. Schwarzenegger had expanded his star persona so that he was now no longer simply an action hero, but one, like Bruce Willis, who brought a hefty dose of comedy to those roles. In Schwarzenegger vehicles like *Kindergarten Cop* (1990), *The Last Action Hero* (1993), and *Junior* (1994, released in the fall after the summer release of *True Lies*), the comedy supersedes the action element. The shift in tone and genre does not mean Cameron is any less invested in reflexive visual technologies – indeed, it's possible that in a more comedic context, some of them take on a new element of sadism, or at least menace, that they had not previously had.

Schwarzenegger had never before been "domesticated" in a Cameron film, though the comedy to be generated from that framework had reaped rewards for other directors. Here he is Secret Agent Harry Tasker, whose work is so secret that his wife Helen (Jamie Lee Curtis) thinks he is a boring computer salesman. The double narrative centers on Harry's foiling of an Arab terrorist ring and Helen's gradual understanding of what her husband does, and her potential relation to it. The opening sequence is meant to show the audience a typical assignment for the secret agent. But it also shows the spectator a panoply of mediating visual technologies, which by now function almost as Cameron's directorial signature. Before the opening credits are finished, Cameron offers up an authorially reflexive moment. Harry Tasker is deep in Lake Chapeau, in full scuba gear, making an altogether unauthorized entrance into a swank party hosted by a questionable

FIGURE 3.6 Schwarzenegger's formal wear refers to Sean Connery's James Bond, one of many intertextual references in *True Lies*.
Lightstorm / 20th Century Fox / The Kobal collection / Rosenthal, Zade

political figure by cutting through an underwater iron gate, and removing his underwater wear to reveal a dinner suit.[10] This is a direct quotation of James Bond (Sean Connery) in *Goldfinger* (1964), and, though unquestionably organic to the plot, it is also clearly a reminder of Cameron's last film, *The Abyss*. That the film begins in German-speaking Switzerland also naturalizes Schwarzenegger's place in it, since he works for a United States spy agency – though by this point in his career that would hardly seem necessary.

Having successfully made it to shore and to the estate, Harry speaks into his walkie-talkie: "Honey, I'm home." This domestic utterance is received not by his wife, but by his working partner Gibson (Tom Arnold), who sits in a van full of surveillance equipment several hundred meters away. The mediated visual technology begins in earnest here, as Gibson gives Harry vital information that he cannot see, but that Gibson can see through night-sight lenses, shown to the audience in a kind of infragreen, suggesting that, as opposed to all of the infrared in previous Cameron films, we are now watching an action film hybridized not with science fiction but with something else. Not only can Gibson see the lay of the land, he can also see Harry, crouched behind an outbuilding. As Gibson describes what he sees to Harry, we see it from his point of view – mediated, technologized, and green – which is to say the point of view of the technology itself. Cameron offers a reverse shot of Gibson, but rather than his face, we're given a close up of a giant telephoto camera lens, banks of monitors in the background, slightly out of focus. The human eye-body is once again joined to technology. Very much as Gorman and Ripley do in *Aliens* and as Lindsey does in *The Abyss*, Cameron assigns Gibson directorial functions, describing for Harry the lay of the land, and telling him where to go and how to get there. Throughout the scene Harry will be by turns responsive and resistant to direction.

Once inside, Harry hacks into a computer, transmitting the data to Gibson's assistant tech-geek Faisil (Grant Heslov, playing the token "good Arab") to download, giving the viewer a shot of computer data that is by now regulation in a Cameron film. Harry's exit from this room is enabled by very low-tech visual technology – a dentist's mirror that reflects Harry's eye to the spectator, and allows Harry to see what's in the hallway without exposing himself. Moments later, he meets the film's femme fatale, Juno Skinner (Tia Carrere). Gibson and Faisil can only hear the two making introductions, so Gibson turns to a computer to generate an image and information about Skinner. Her photo and vital statistics are shown to Gibson and the audience on a computer screen, recalling the way the crew of the Nostromo was represented in Aliens.

The estate's guards discover a security breach, and they gradually make their way to Harry, who is by now doing a tango with Skinner. That the next part of the sequence turns on Harry's ignoring Gibson's entreaties – his direction – to vacate establishes the comedic thread of True Lies. In previous films, none of them comedies, all such directions have been followed to the letter. When the James Bond-style escape sequence begins, the framework of mediated technology is suspended in favor of very traditional crosscutting between the pursued Harry and Gibson and Faisil racing to the rendezvous point.

In True Lies mediated visual technology is also a sure sign of the professional and public spheres – as it generally is in Cameron's other films. The Terminator is nothing but his profession, at least in the first film, and that means he is entirely reliant on his visual field to give him the data needed to get the job done. The Marines in Aliens rely on their video and vital signs equipment only in working situations, and this is also true of the engineers on the oilrig in The Abyss. Cameron reinforces Harry's disengagement from his family and his over-engagement in his work in two ways. Comically, he displaces all of the domestic clichés onto Harry and Gibson rather than Harry and Helen. "Honey, I'm home," says Harry to his partner when he breaches the estate. "Thanks, dear," when Gibson, who comes and goes to and from Harry's home as if he, too, we a family member, offers him a cup of coffee in the Tasker kitchen. But, just as Cameron allows the domestic discourse to permeate Harry and Gibson's professional life (also giving their relationship a completely disingenuous homoerotic edge), he also allows the professional visual technology into the domestic sphere. Indeed, it is this very technology that both incites Harry's desire to square the two sides of his life, and also provides the means to do it. The morning after Harry and Gibson return from Switzerland, they stand in Harry's kitchen, and Gibson demonstrates to him the latest spywear: sunglasses that actually transmit video images from a camera disguised in a cigarette pack. One can hardly imagine a more self-highlighting gesture than a pair of glasses – already a visual aid – with another visual enhancer built into it. Certainly the added visual information from the surveillance camera will reduce information seen through the lens of the glasses, reminding us that the act of seeing a movie requires that we start with an uninterrupted field of light and, in the interest of viewing an image, need to see a reduction in that light (the filmstrip passing over the light source) if we want to be informed and entertained.[11]

Harry holds the glasses, his point of view showing us their interior, on which plays a crude image of Harry's own living room. When he puts them on, he is treated to a "movie" of his daughter Dana (Eliza Dushku) stealing money from his wallet. Now that his eye is so close to the screen image inside the glass, his own point of view and that of the surveillance camera become one and the same (reminding us, by way of star intertext, of Schwarzenegger's mechanized vision as the Terminator – and the style of glasses is also meant to recall the Gargoyles worn by the cyborg in the earlier film), and we see Dana's theft of the money in grainy greyish tones, just like a store surveillance camera designed to pick up exactly this kind of criminal activity – but certainly not intended to document it in the private, domestic sphere.

The interpenetration of public and private, technologized and organic continues as Harry and Gibson have a "kids today" conversation as they head into work at the Omega Sector, "The Last Line of Defense." Discussions about Dana's sexual activity, real or imagined, and the unfaithfulness of Gibson's wife take place as the two men are followed by surveillance cameras, scanned for weapons, and identify themselves with voice recognition technology and retinal scans, their data portraits in the way of hand X-rays and ultrasounds of their eyeballs, as well as a field of textual and numerical data, showing on video screens for the viewer to see. At no point in their work environment are they out of sight of surveillance technology or computer screens with images and data readouts, and most of the time they are depicted in the act of using all of these things, professional necessities that define their public selves. Time and again as Harry and Gibson try to stop the Crimson Jihad, a terrorist ring,[12] they rely on screen images and screen technologies to do it, from databank photos on computer screens, to surveillance video replayed larger than life behind them at Omega headquarters, to the state-of-the-art spy technology that literally gives Harry eyes in the back of his head. All of these images come to the viewer as frames within the film frame.

This interpenetration climaxes just over an hour into *True Lies*. Harry, thinking that Helen is having an affair, decides to put her under surveillance using wiretapping, Global Positioning, bugging, tailing, and infrared helicopter pursuit. Finding her through these technologies, he and his Omega team abduct her from her tryst with a used car salesman ((Bill Paxton) who, as a seduction shtick, poses as a secret agent). They bring her to their headquarters to interrogate her using secret agent methods that emphasize mediated vision as well. This interrogation scene, eight minutes in length, recalls the police and psychiatric evaluations from *The Terminator* and T2. Helen stands alone in a large cement-walled room with a two-way mirror in front of her. As she looks at her own image in the large glass (rectangular like a widescreen film screen), trying to discern who sits behind it, Cameron cuts to a reverse shot in which we can not only see Helen from the other side of the mirror, but her image on closed circuit video feed on a monitor positioned inside the mirror frame, as well as the cameras providing the image, offering us both the "real" Helen and the moving-image Helen – though, again, neither image is actually real. The camera tracks back to reveal a comprehensive battery of monitoring devices, a ramped-up version of what Cameron revealed at the end of Sarah Connor's evaluation scene in T2. Using voice distortion technology to shield his identity, Harry interrogates his wife, his menacing commands coming through to Helen like the voice of God.

As Harry questions her (just as he would one of the terrorists he is chasing), Gibson activates one of the surveillance monitors to show not just a video image of Helen, but a heat-sensor scan of her face in close up. This larger monitor sits on top of two smaller ones showing her conventional video image. Throughout the interrogation, Harry and Gibson will pay these monitors little mind; they are primarily offered for audience consumption, offering confirmation of Helen's emotional intensity and commitment to her husband, an aspect of her character it will take Harry slightly longer to grasp. As in *The Terminator*, the images are often doubled as they reflect off the glass, showing as many as seven different images of Helen at any given moment, reminding us of the infinite repeatability of the cinematic image as a mass-produced, distributed, exhibited and received commodity. The questions shift from her professional involvement with an alleged secret agent to questions about her personal life and her marriage. When repeatedly questioned about whether she has been unfaithful to Harry (she has not), Helen's response is to take the stool she's been sitting on and to smash the two-way mirror with it, cracking the glass, though not breaking through to the other side. This is the first time in a Cameron film that the mirror or screen (or both) in such a scene has been compromised in any way. Helen looks at a distorted version of herself in the mirror. The irony, of course, is that it is through these intensely mediated visual technologies and multiplied images that Harry and Helen begin to rediscover their connection to each other, rendering *True Lies* not just a comedy, but, in particular, a remarriage comedy.[13] As the couple reunites toward the end of the film after an extended action sequence in which both behave like action heroes, Harry replaces Helen's wedding ring on her finger and they kiss, renewing their vows as a nuclear weapon detonates in the ocean behind them – restoring the nuclear family in more than one way.

TITANIC (1997)

Titanic, Cameron's most expensive and most successful film to date, is the work that seems, on the face of it, to invest less in mediated technologies of seeing than any previous Cameron project. After all, it is largely a period piece – there are no possibilities for video surveillance, motion sensors, infrared, or computer technology here. Generically it is a romance[14] that accelerates into an action film – or, as Cameron described it, "you've got a two-hour movie that's all about people, and then the effects movie starts."[15] Over the three-hour-plus epic, the present-tense framing narrative seems relatively unobtrusive, though it functions at crucial times in vital ways (see below). But there are strong indications from the very first frame of Titanic that Cameron has sustained his preoccupations with visual technology.

Before the spectator sees anything, Titanic begins as an aural experience, its ethereal, haunting Enya-esque theme music[16] (non-verbal, but sung by a person, Sissel Kyrkjebo, and not to be confused with Celine Dion's chest-thumping, exorcism-worthy theme song) playing over a black screen for brief seconds before the first image, as if to clear the viewer's mind of the long line of splashy trailers she has just seen. The first image reveals Cameron's investment in a commodified version of history (see my Introduction). The black screen dissolves into a sepia-toned image of hundreds of people on the dock waving at the Titanic. The camera pans up and left, and we apprehend the enormity, the majesty, and the scale of the vessel. The theme continues to play as this first shot dissolves into one from the point of view of someone on the dock. This shot tracks screen left, and for a moment we have a doubled reflexivity. The sepia tone and slightly jerky, slightly slow motion suggest to us that this is old footage (which would have been shot at 16 frames per second instead of 24), even real and therefore documentary or news footage, giving it a stronger weight of truth and history – never mind that widescreen technologies did not exist in 1912. In this second shot we also see a cameraman cranking his camera, documenting the Titanic. This cameraman is none other than James Cameron himself, providing an Alfred Hitchcock-like cameo (though nowhere near as showy as Hitchcock's were). The director shooting the shot is in the shot shooting another shot, and the Titanic is the object of (the appearance of) layered representation.[17] But the reflexivity is less in the service of authorship per se, and more in the service of thickening the discourse of historical accuracy so vital to the film's success. These four sepia-toned shots dissolve into a black, moonlit ocean on which the title "Titanic" appears. This image dissolves, and for a moment the spectator might be reminded of *The Abyss*, as the timeless ocean shot is cut with one of two deep sea submersibles diving down into the sea, the faint diegetic sound of their sonar competing with the lilting tune. They disappear into blackness. For the first time a cut is abrupt, and we are presented with a full frontal shot of the submersibles, the engine noise coming from them, and no soundtrack. In seven shots and fewer than two minutes, Cameron has sutured together the past with the present in such a way that the spectator will seamlessly move back and forth between them, though it might be more accurate to say that Cameron will move the spectator seamlessly (and authoritatively) back and forth between them. This mini-opening is a compacted version of what is to come when Rose (Gloria Stuart) begins to tell her story, a story that generates the rest of *Titanic*'s narrative.

For the next several minutes, Cameron submerges us in the present day, as the technology necessary to locate, reach, explore and make images of the ocean liner are foregrounded (much of it visual mapping technology, including radar and video), and the Titanic itself, where most of the rest of the film will transpire, exists not as a location, but instead as a specular object. Titanic hunter Brock Lovett (Bill Paxton) and his crew sit inside the submersible Mir One and carefully navigate the surface of the ship. In the background of most shots are screens that, but for content, look little different from the video screens and monitors of *Aliens*, *The Abyss*, *True Lies* or either *Terminator* film. The crew sends out remote operated vehicles (ROVs) with video feed to survey the interior of the ship. The ROVs emphasize their historical distance from the ship and from 1912 not only in their technology, but also in name: Dunkin', which describes precisely what the ROV does (dunks deep into the ocean), and Snoop Dog, which jokingly refers not only to its size and its mission, but also to a current-day rap artist. The ROVs can go where the explorers cannot, and they function as the explorers' eyes. Cameron produces this vision for the spectator in ways completely consistent with all of his earlier films. He alternates shots of the interiors of the Mir and the Titanic, the ship now dark, covered in sludge and barnacles, sand drifting through its crevices and openings, and over the personal objects left behind by its victims – a doll's head, a shoe, and, most reflexively, a pair of eyeglasses. But within that pattern, the views of the ship are just as often from the point of view of Dunkin' and Snoop Dog as from Cameron's omniscient camera. The spectator thus gets both a more colorful version of the ship's interior from Cameron's lens, and an almost black and white, slightly pixilated version from the ROVs. Again veering almost into a familiar Cameronian paradox, the state-of-the-art imaging technology produced by the ROVs reminds us of nothing so much as the equally monochrome and slightly imperfect sepia images from the start of the film, thus folding the historical past into the absolute present. In case the spectator has missed this metavisual paradigm, Cameron offers up one framing of Snoop Dog's point of view, as seen on the video monitor inside the Mir, with a caption on the bottom right of the frame that reads "Left Eye."

Further manifesting Cameron's extraordinary consistency in this string of shots is the way the working of the ROVs and their metavisual technology repeat the tropes of film direction, just as in *Aliens* and *True Lies*, where those who are physically joined to the technology are directed by someone else in the use of it. In this case, Lewis Bodine (Lewis Abernathy) wears what looks like the kind of headgear used for Virtual Reality games, or even IMAX movies – it is labeled "Snoop Vision" – and steers Snoop Dog, which is to say operates the camera, according to Lovett's direction. "Hold it, hold it . . . go up to the right," and so on. Lovett, by Cameron's own admission, is intended to be seen as a stand-in for the director, making this the most direct reference to Cameron as a filmmaker in any of his films. When Lovett guesses the safe that contains the giant "Heart of the Ocean" diamond might be under a piece of furniture, he instructs Bodine to explore. This cannot be done with a mere zoom, and so Bodine takes out his "hands," and, recalling Ripley in the loader in *Aliens*, manipulates the ROV's pincers by putting his hands inside two similar tools inside the Mir.

All of this could be considered an accidental representation of Cameron's preoccupation with vision – accidental insofar as every one of the events serves the story line quite directly. What follows does not, and is among the densest representations of representation and spectatorship in the film. The safe has been emptied and the diamond, disappointingly, not found. From a makeshift lab on the Keldysh, the ship that is home base to the Titanic exploration, Lovett placates unhappy investors via telephone. As he does, white coated lab technicians carefully rinse off the soggy paper found in the safe. This task is documented by a video camera hanging over the basin, which feeds live to a monitor just behind the technicians. As Jack Dawson's drawing of the naked young Rose, wearing nothing but the Heart of the Ocean, becomes visible to us, we first see the sludge clearing with an unmediated shot into the basin. Rose's face becomes visible first (imitating a cinematic close-up), then the rest of her. But Lovett sees the unveiling on the video monitor – he does not apprehend the actual drawing. Needing to confirm what he sees, he grabs a photograph of the Heart of the Ocean and holds it next to the drawing. At one point this is shown to us with the actual drawing as photograph in the foreground, and the video image of the drawing and photograph in the background (centered in the frame). Clearly, in the absence of the real diamond, an object that will be the impetus for so much of the action (and the ideology) of *Titanic*, we are offered a multitude of representations of it. But in this instance, we get the familiar representation of a representation (in this case of an absent object and an absent person, both of which will become present) – a thickened *mise en abyme* that reaffirms the film's interest in the matrices of representation, history and commodification. But more: this sequence recalls nothing so much as the various interrogation scenes of *The Terminator*, *Terminator 2*, and *True Lies*. And this suggests that, though she has not even yet been named, let alone located and brought to the ship, Rose is already under some form of interrogation, if only by Cameron and the cinematic apparatus itself.

This image of Rose is cut with one of a table on which sit several framed photographs, all of them old, all black and white, one of them of a woman sitting on an elephant, suggesting the subject of the photos is not your average woman. If the scene transition here is smooth insofar as we move from one set of photographic representations to another, it is abrupt insofar as we move from the high-tech, low-comfort, marine-based world of the ship to a land-based, cozy, almost Bohemian home and studio, where the television and the telephone are the most technologically advanced objects, and neither is state of the art. But the scenes mirror each other in a way. The lush plant life of the deep ocean is echoed in the lush plant life of the house and garden. The sea life is matched by a goldfish bowl, and even Snoop Dog has a double in a lively Pomeranian. As we have just seen the technicians hunched over washing what looks like red clay off the drawing of Rose, so we now see Rose herself hunched over a potter's wheel working with red clay, her real hands covered in just the same liquid as her image was moments ago. As Rose hears Brock Lovett on television repeatedly utter the word "Titanic," her attention turns to the source. We are given Rose's point of view looking at the very small TV screen through a glass door on which is reflected the room she is in, and the outside. She walks inside to pay closer attention, and, just as Lovett has seen Rose's image, so Rose now beholds Lovett's, framed side by side with the anchorwoman who is interviewing him via satellite, the two frames sitting within the television frame sitting within the film frame. As the interview goes on, Lovett refers to the drawing, and the TV camera tilts down to display it, floating clean in the water. Thus Rose firsts re-encounters her image qua image, just as Lovett did, on a TV screen rather than the thing itself. As the TV camera moves in to offer a close-up of the drawing (again repeating the pattern of the previous scene), Cameron does the same on the old Rose. Her response is identical to Lovett's, "I'll be Goddamned." The scene concludes as Rose calls Lovett to identify herself, saying, "the woman in the picture is me." It is not without interest that Cameron then cuts dramatically to a frame filled with nothing but buoyant ocean, and orchestral music to go with it, an image that recalls the title shot, but its daylight (and, because of the music, its mood) is the opposite. Eventually entering into this frame is the helicopter carrying Rose to the Keldysh, where she will tell her story to Lovett and, because this is a big-budget James Cameron epic, to the world. The "real" narrative of *Titanic* may now begin.

Almost. Rose still needs to take control of the narrative reins, and, once again, Cameron uses mediating visual technology to make this transition. After Rose views her drawing, as well as several effects recovered from her stateroom, including a butterfly hair-comb and a hand-held mirror ("The reflection has changed a bit," she muses), Lovett asks her a question whose awkwardness reveals an important mechanism of the film. Kneeling behind her, he gently asks her, "Are you ready to go back to Titanic?" She quietly and emotionally nods. Now, clearly, Rose cannot go back to Titanic physically – she is not hardy enough even to go down in a submersible. And even if she could, the temporal element of the passage of decades means that she cannot go back in time, either. Of course, this is precisely what cinematic flashbacks *can* do. But Cameron does not offer us any typical

FIGURE 3.7 Rose examines her effects, observed by multiple cameras.
20th Century Fox / Paramount / The Kobal collection / Wallace, Merie W.

form of flashback. He does not signal it with the dreamy harp music and wavy or dissolving frames so familiar from hundreds of other films. Rather, he collapses space and time by transforming one image into another, rather than replacing one image with another.

Because *Titanic* will henceforth be told from one person's point of view and with one person's narrative authority, and because the events are so chaotic, Cameron pauses one last time to use mediated visual technology to tell the entire story of the sinking (from an engineering, not a personal, perspective). This technology is both a contrast with and a gateway to a time when none of said technology existed, and when human ocular perception was very different, the high and simultaneously varied speeds of modernity just taking hold in Western cultures. From this three-shot of Lovett, Rose, and Rose's granddaughter Lizzie (Suzy Amis), soft piano music playing on the soundtrack, Cameron cuts to Bodine, who loudly and without any sympathy, sensitivity or feeling for Rose's predicament, narrates a computer generated animation of the sinking of the Titanic, which Rose watches composed, but deeply rattled. As she watches the submersibles video feeds, her own memories interrupt those images in the form of flash cuts, a different perspective on those same locations.

In the editing of the scene, which alternates among shots of the computer animation (briefly adding cartoon to *Titanic*'s genre mix), Rose watching, Bodine narrating, and stoic reaction shots of Rose, another effect becomes clear: for all that Rose witnessed the disaster, for all that she was a participant in the events of the sinking, she was not at any time – could not have been – a spectator in the sense that she is when presented with the film-within-a-film of the Titanic sinking. During these moments, she is a passive, even abject spectator, helpless not only because she can do nothing but watch the display, but also because the events re-enacted before her (and re-enacted yet again for the rest of the film) have already happened. But that is soon to change.

Rose activates herself as a narrator by activating herself as a spectator. After seeing the computer model and disputing not the fact of it but its feeling, she is asked by Lovett to share her story. She rises from

her wheelchair and walks to a bank of live feed video monitors showing images sent back by Dunkin' and Snoop Dog, the ROVs. As she
looks at the decomposing ship, she can also see her own image
reflected on the glass of the monitors. This double vision literally places
her back on the ship, at least within the video frame (and, of course,
the film frame that contains it). As she gazes emotionally on the submerged forms, her memory is flash cut into them, full, vibrant, incan-
descently lit color replacing the monochromatic, dark, wet versions of
these same objects and spaces. These are cuts we can clearly see and
register as cuts.[18] Subsequently, Rose begins to narrate specifically in
terms of vivid sense memory: "It's been 84 years . . . and I can still
smell the fresh paint. The china had never been used. The sheets had
never been slept in." As she speaks, the camera holds her in a close-up,
an image of the Titanic's bow visible in the background on a video
monitor, mediated visual technology once again reminding us that we
are in the realm of memory, history, cinema. It dollies in so that her
face fills the frame, excising all other visual evidence and technologies.
A soft, lilting piano theme begins to play that we have not previously
heard. There is nothing but Rose, her speech (memory and narrative)
and a soundtrack that cues us to reflect and feel a certain poignancy in
her words.

Rose then says "Titanic was called 'the Ship of Dreams.'" At this
point the camera rotates around screen right to reintroduce the video
screen with the bow of the ship on it. This image will now hold a profoundly different value for the spectator. As she continues, "and it was.
It really was," her face goes out of focus, she slips out of frame (still
audible) and the camera moves past her to the image of Titanic's bow.
Imperceptibly, the video image ceases to be bound by the confines of
the monitor and becomes a regular widescreen shot. But this shot is an
extraordinary one. As the camera continues to move screen right, the
ship reverses in time, and space, gradually morphing from its dark,
submarine grave to its broad daylight, majestic, brand-new self, docked
in Southampton. This morph, 21 minutes into the film, contrasts
starkly with Rose's previous memory of the ship, whose images

intruded and competed with those she observed on the video screen. Here the transition is seamless, as well as impossible. Cameron has not only turned the narrative authority of the film firmly over to Rose in this shot, he has also firmly reminded the audience of cinema's particular space-time capacities. After several shots of the hustle and bustle of the embarking passengers and crew, we reencounter Rose getting out of a chauffeur-driven automobile. She is now her younger self (Kate Winslet), and she looks up at the ship from under the wide brim of a hat, thoroughly unimpressed. As they embark, the older Rose describes her unhappy predicament in voiceover, unifying the two realms once again. Just after this, at 24 minutes, we are introduced to Jack Dawson.

When the narrative concludes (there will be the recounting of the dénouement, but the climax is over), Cameron returns to a shot of old Rose. But it is an extreme close-up of her closed eyes – a kind of soft inversion of the close-up of Jack's eyes as recalled by Rose when she first sees his drawing of her on the Keldysh. When Bodine tells her that

FIGURE 3.8 The Titanic, its past rendered present by Rose's narrative and Cameron's camera.
20th Century Fox / Paramount / The Kobal collection / Wallace, Merie W.

there is no record of anyone named Jack, she says she doesn't even have a picture of him. The audience, on the other hand, has thousands of pictures of Jack in the form of film frames. Bodine may remain doubtful, but we believe Rose. And after she throws overboard the Heart of the Ocean, which she has been secreting these many decades, she returns to her room, and Cameron finally lets us see the images of images from a time before video surveillance – the photograph. Those pictures that we saw only fleetingly at the beginning of the film are offered up to us now to peruse at some leisure: Rose as actress, aviator, elephant- and horseback-rider – each could itself be a still from a Classical Hollywood film. If these are images of Rose as a specular object, and reflexively framed within the film frame, the very last images bring us back to Rose's interiority, though this is clearly a dream (the other category besides memory with which cinema so powerfully resonates), and possibly a dream before dying. Once again we see an effects shot in which the submerged Titanic gradually becomes its former splendid self, as Rose glides along the halls to the grand staircase. It seems that all 1500 passengers and crew are reassembled there, no longer divided by first class, staff and steerage, and as the camera maintains her physical point of view, she mounts the stairs to a waiting Jack. But, as Jack reaches out his hand to Rose, Cameron pulls away from Rose's point of view, restoring an omniscient camera as we see the couple reunited (to thunderous applause and music designed to make the spectator weep) for the romantic Hollywood kiss ending.

Titanic is the latest and least expected of Cameron's meta-visually structured films, but it is very much in line with his others in this sense – though it is certainly amusing to think of Gloria Stuart's tender Rose and Arnold Schwarzenegger's ruthless Terminator as belonging to the same cinematic paradigm. And yet they do, each – and every narrative in between – bearing very consistent marks not only of Cameron's interest in vision and visuality, but also of the unmistakable ways in which he produces that interest for the viewer, time and again.

4

JAMES CAMERON CHRONOLOGY

History	Culture	Film Culture	Cameron Biography
		(Film titles in bold indicate Academy Award for best picture)	

1954

U.S. Supreme Court decision on Brown v. Board of Education		**On the Waterfront** *Rear Window* *Them!* *La Strada* *Carmen Jones* *Seven Samurai* Roger Corman produces first film, *The Fast and the Furious*	James Cameron born August 16 in Kapuskasing, Ontario, Canada

1955

Rosa Parks refuses to give up her seat on a bus	Disneyland opens James Dean dies in car accident McDonald's Corporation founded	**Marty** *Rebel without a Cause* *The Night of the Hunter* *Smiles of a Summer Night* *The Man with the Golden Arm* *Pather Panchali*	

History	Culture	Film Culture	Cameron Biography
		(Film titles in bold indicate Academy Award for best picture)	

1956

| | | ***Around the World in 80 Days*** | |

1957

| | | ***The Bridge on the River Kwai*** | |

1958

| Chinese leader Mao Zedong launches the "Great Leap Forward"

NASA founded | Hula hoops become popular

Lego toy bricks first introduced | ***Gigi***
Touch of Evil
Look Back in Anger | |

1959

| Fidel Castro becomes leader of Cuba

International treaty makes Antarctica scientific preserve

Nixon & Khrushchev's "Kitchen Debate" | | **Ben Hur** nominated for 12 Academy Awards. It wins 11, including Best Picture, setting a record that will not even be tied until *Titanic*.
Imitation of Life
The 400 Blows
Room at the Top
Rio Bravo | Cameron family moves to Niagara Falls, Ontario |

1960

| First televised presidential debates

Civil rights sit-in at Woolworth's in Greensborough, South Carolina | Lasers invented | ***The Apartment***
Psycho
Peeping Tom
La Dolce Vita
Breathless
L'Avventura
The Magnificent Seven | |

History	Culture	Film Culture	Cameron Biography
		(Film titles in bold indicate Academy Award for best picture)	

1961

Adolf Eichmann on trial for role in Holocaust		**West Side Story**	
		Last Year at Marienbad	
		Breakfast at Tiffany's	
Bay of Pigs invasion		*Judgment at Nuremburg*	
		The Children's Hour	
Berlin Wall built			
Peace Corps founded			
Soviets launch first man in space			

1962

Cuban Missile Crisis	Death of Marilyn Monroe	**Lawrence of Arabia**	
		The Manchurian Candidate	
First person killed trying to cross the Berlin Wall	Andy Warhol's Campbell's Soup Can exhibited	*Jules and Jim*	
		The Man Who Shot Liberty Valance	
		Knife in the Water	

1963

John F. Kennedy assassinated	Betty Friedan publishes *The Feminine Mystique*	**Tom Jones**	
		8½	
Martin Luther King Jr. delivers "I Have a Dream" speech		*Contempt*	
		The Birds	
		Cleopatra	

1964

Civil Rights Act passes in U.S.	Cassius Clay (a.k.a. Muhammad Ali) becomes World Heavyweight Champion	**My Fair Lady**	
		A Hard Day's Night	
Nelson Mandela sentenced to life in prison		*Woman in the Dunes*	
		Goldfinger	
Warren Commission issues report on JFK's assassination	Beatles play first U.S. shows	*Dr. Strangelove, Or, How I learned to Stop Worrying and Love the Bomb*	
		A Fistful of Dollars	

History	Culture	Film Culture	Cameron Biography
		(Film titles in bold indicate Academy Award for best picture)	

1965

Los Angeles riots	Japan's bullet train opens	**The Sound of Music**	James Cameron
Malcolm X assassinated	New York City Great Blackout	*Alphaville*	and family move
U.S. sends troops to Vietnam		*Repulsion*	to Chippewa, near
		Darling	Niagara Falls,
		Help!	Ontario

1966

Black Panther Party established	Star Trek T.V. series airs	**A Man for All Seasons**	
Mao Zedong launches the Cultural Revolution		*Persona*	
		Blow Up	
		Closely Watched Trains	
Mass protests against the draft in U.S.		*Black Girl*	

1967

Che Guevara killed	First heart transplant	*In the Heat of the Night*	
Six Day War in the Middle East	First Super Bowl	*Belle du Jour*	
	Stalin's daughter defects	*Weekend*	
		In Cold Blood	
	Three U.S. astronauts killed during simulated launch	*The Graduate*	
		Bonnie and Clyde	
		Guess Who's Coming to Dinner?	

1968

Martin Luther King Jr. assassinated		**Oliver!**	
		The Producers	
Prague Spring		*Planet of the Apes*	
Student and worker protests in Paris, Mexico City and elsewhere		*Night of the Living Dead*	
		Memories of Underdevelopment	

History	Culture	Film Culture	Cameron Biography
		(Film titles in bold indicate Academy Award for best picture)	

1968 (continued)

History	Culture	Film Culture	Cameron Biography
Protests at the Democratic National Convention in Chicago Robert F. Kennedy assassinated Tet Offensive		2001: *A Space Odyssey* (Cameron views this film ten times in its opening weeks)	

1969

History	Culture	Film Culture	Cameron Biography
Neil Armstrong becomes the first man on the moon Yasser Arafat becomes leader of P.L.O.	ARPANET, the precursor of the Internet, created Charles Manson and "Family" Arrested Rock-and-roll concert at Woodstock	**Midnight Cowboy** *Medium Cool* *Easy Rider* *Butch Cassidy and the Sundance Kid*	Cameron makes amateur film *Niagara, or How I Learned to Stop Worrying and Love the Falls*

1970

History	Culture	Film Culture	Cameron Biography
American soldiers accused of murdering entire town of Vietnamese civilians Protesting students at Kent State shot, four killed	Aswan High Dam completed Beatles break-up Computer floppy disks introduced	**Patton** *M*A*S*H* *The Rolling Stones: Gimme Shelter* *The Conformist* *Little Big Man* *Airport*	

1971

History	Culture	Film Culture	Cameron Biography
	VCRs introduced "All in the Family" debuts	**The French Connection** *McCabe and Mrs. Miller* *The Last Picture Show* *Dirty Harry* *A Clockwork Orange*	Cameron and family move to Orange County, California

History	Culture	Film Culture	Cameron Biography
		(Film titles in bold indicate Academy Award for best picture)	

1972

History	Culture	Film Culture	Cameron Biography
Watergate break-in and scandal Terrorist attack at the Olympic Games in Munich	M*A*S*H T.V. shows premiers Pocket calculators introduced	**The Godfather** The Discreet Charm of the Bourgeoisie Deliverance Cries and Whispers The Ruling Class Cabaret	Cameron sees Dr. Zhivago (1965) for the first time. Like 2001, it has a profound effect on him. Cameron meets Sharon Williams.

1973

History	Culture	Film Culture	Cameron Biography
U.S. pulls out of Vietnam Roe v. Wade settled U.S. Vice-President Spiro Agnew resigns		**The Sting** Mean Streets The Exorcist Badlands American Graffiti Sleeper	Cameron enrolls in Fullerton College. Cameron and Sharon Williams move in together.

1974

History	Culture	Film Culture	Cameron Biography
Halie Selassie, emperor of Ethiopia, deposed U.S. President Richard Nixon resigns	Mikhail Baryshnikov defects Patty Hearst kidnapped by Symbionese Liberation Army	**The Godfather Part II** The Conversation A Woman under the Influence Monty Python and the Holy Grail Chinatown Blazing Saddles	Cameron drops out of Fullerton College.

1975

History	Culture	Film Culture	Cameron Biography
President Gerald Ford pardons former president Richard Nixon Civil war in Lebanon Pol Pot becomes the Communist dictator of Cambodia	Arthur Ashe first black man to win Wimbledon Microsoft founded	**One Flew over the Cuckoo's Nest** Nashville Jaws Shampoo Dog Day Afternoon The Rocky Horror Picture Show	Cameron quits his job as a school bus and truck driver in Orange County.

History	Culture	Film Culture	Cameron Biography
		(Film titles in bold indicate Academy Award for best picture)	

1976

North and South Vietnam join to form the Socialist Republic of Vietnam	Nadia Comaneci given seven perfect tens at Olympics	**Rocky** *Taxi Driver* *Network* *The Outlaw Josey Wales* *All the President's Men*	
United States celebrates bicentennial			

1977

South African anti-apartheid leader Steve Biko tortured to death	Elvis found dead Miniseries *Roots* airs	**Annie Hall** *Saturday Night Fever* *Star Wars* *Close Encounters of the Third Kind*	James Cameron marries Sharon Williams.

1978

John Paul II becomes pope Jonestown Massacre	First test-tube baby born *Dallas* TV series debuts	**The Deer Hunter** *Halloween* *Grease* *Days of Heaven* *Superman: The Movie*	Cameron goes to work for Roger Corman's New World Pictures.

1979

Ayatollah Khomeini returns as leader of Iran Iran takes American hostages in Tehran	*Holocaust* miniseries airs Sony introduces the Walkman	**Kramer vs. Kramer** *Manhattan* *Apocalypse Now* *Alien* *Norma Rae* *Mad Max* *The China Syndrome*	
Margaret Thatcher becomes first woman prime minister of Great Britain			
Nuclear accident at Three Mile Island			

History	Culture	Film Culture	Cameron Biography
		(Film titles in bold indicate Academy Award for best picture)	

1980

Ronald Reagan elected president of the United States Mount St. Helens erupts in Washington State	John Lennon assassinated Rubik's Cube popular Ted Turner establishes CNN (Cable News Network)	**Ordinary People** *Raging Bull* *The Empire Strikes Back* *The Shining* *Airplane!*	James Cameron is Art Director for Roger Corman's *Battle Beyond the Stars* (written by John Sayles)

1981

Assassination attempt on U.S. President Reagan by John Hinckley Sandra Day O'Connor, first woman appointed to the U.S. Supreme Court AIDS identified and named	IBM introduces personal computers (PCs)	**Chariots of Fire** *Das Boot* *Reds* *My Dinner with Andre* *Pixote*	

1982

Falkland Islands/ Malvinas War between Great Britain and Argentina	Channel Four in the U.K. launched Michael Jackson releases *Thriller* Reverend Sun Myung Moon marries 2,075 couples at Madison Square Garden	**Gandhi** *Blade Runner* *Diner* *E.T. The Extra-Terrestrial* *Fast Times at Ridgemont High* *Koyaanisqatsi*	Cameron directs *Piranha 2: The Spawning*

History	Culture	Film Culture	Cameron Biography
		(Film titles in bold indicate Academy Award for best picture)	

1983

Reagan announces defense plan called Star Wars Soviets shoot down Korean airliner U.S. Embassy in Beirut bombed	Sally Ride becomes first American woman in space	**Terms of Endearment** *The Big Chill* *The Right Stuff* *Paris, Texas* *Silkwood* *Scarface* *Risky Business*	

1984

Huge poison gas leak in Bhopal, India Indian Prime Minister Indira Gandhi assassinated by two bodyguards	PG-13 Movie rating created Vietnam War Memorial opened in Washington, D.C.	**Amadeus** *Once Upon a Time in America* *Blood Simple* *A Nightmare on Elm Street* *Repo Man*	James Cameron directs *The Terminator* Cameron divorces Sharon Williams (on whom the character of Sarah Connor in *The Terminator* is loosely based)

1985

Famine in Ethiopia Hole in the ozone layer discovered Mikhail Gorbachev calls for *glasnost* and *perestroika*	New Coke hits the market Wreck of the Titanic found Live Aid concert	**Out of Africa** *Brazil* *The Color Purple* *Back to the Future* *My Beautiful Laundrette* *The Breakfast Club* *Rambo: First Blood Part II* (written by James Cameron)	Cameron marries *Terminator* producer Gale Anne Hurd

1986

Challenger Space Shuttle explodes Chernobyl nuclear accident	*The Cosby Show* debuts	**Platoon** *She's Gotta Have It* *Blue Velvet* *Tampopo* *Sid and Nancy*	*Aliens* is nominated for 7 Academy Awards. It wins 2.

History	Culture	Film Culture	Cameron Biography
		(Film titles in bold indicate Academy Award for best picture)	

1986 (continued)

Ferdinand Marcos flees the Philippines		*Down by Law* *Ferris Bueller's Day Off*	
Iran–Contra scandal unfolds			
U.S. bombs Libya			
U.S.S.R. launches Mir Space Station			

1987

ACT UP (AIDS Coalition to Unleash Power) founded in New York City	DNA first used to convict criminals	**The Last Emperor** *Wings of Desire* *Raising Arizona* *Full Metal Jacket*	
	New York Stock Exchange suffers huge drop on "Black Monday"	*The Princess Bride* *Lethal Weapon* *Dirty Dancing*	
Klaus Barbie, the Nazi Butcher of Lyons, sentenced to life in prison			

1988

George H.W. Bush elected president of the United States		**Rain Man** *The Thin Blue Line* *Die Hard*	Cameron is uncredited writer on *Alien Nation*
Pan Am flight 103 is bombed over Lockerbie		*Women on the Verge of a Nervous Breakdown* *Who Framed Roger Rabbit?*	
U.S. shoots down Iranian airliner		*The Last Temptation of Christ*	

1989

Fall of the Berlin Wall		**Driving Miss Daisy** *Do the Right Thing*	*The Abyss* is nominated for 4 Academy Awards.
Exxon Valdez spills millions of gallons of oil on Alaska coastline		*Sex, lies and videotape* *Drugstore Cowboy* *Heathers*	It wins 1.

History	Culture	Film Culture	Cameron Biography
		(Film titles in bold indicate Academy Award for best picture)	

1989 (continued)

History	Culture	Film Culture	Cameron Biography
Students massacred in China's Tiananmen Square		The Cook, the Thief, His Wife and Her Lover Glory Batman	After divorcing Gale Anne Hurd in February, Cameron marries director Kathryn Bigelow (Near Dark, Point Break, Blue Steel, Strange Days) in August.

1990

History	Culture	Film Culture	Cameron Biography
Hubble Telescope launched into space Lech Walesa becomes first president of Poland Nelson Mandela freed		**Dances with Wolves** Longtime Companion La Femme Nikita Ghost Goodfellas Pretty Woman Edward Scissorhands	Cameron forms his production company, Lightstorm Entertainment

1991

History	Culture	Film Culture	Cameron Biography
Collapse of the Soviet Union Operation Desert Storm South Africa repeals Apartheid Laws		**Silence of the Lambs** Beauty and the Beast Bugsy JFK Boyz 'N the Hood Raise the Red Lantern	Cameron is uncredited writer on Point Break. Terminator 2: Judgment Day opens July 4th. Over half the movie tickets bought in North America that weekend are for the movie. T2 is nominated for 6 Academy Awards. It wins 4. Cameron divorces Kathryn Bigelow.

History	Culture	Film Culture	Cameron Biography
		(Film titles in bold indicate Academy Award for best picture)	

1992

Bill Clinton elected president of the United States Official end of the Cold War Riots and rebellion in Los Angeles after the Rodney King verdict	Madonna's *Sex* book	**Unforgiven** *Malcolm X* *The Crying Game* *The Player* *El Mariachi* *Basic Instinct*	Linda Hamilton gives birth to Josephine Cameron, James Cameron's first child.

1993

Cult compound in Waco, Texas raided World Trade Center bombed	Use of the Internet grows exponentially	**Schindler's List** *The Piano* *The Remains of the Day* *Groundhog Day* *Menace II Society* *Philadelphia* *The Age of Innocence*	Cameron founds Digital Domain, a special-effects company.

1994

Nelson Mandela elected president of South Africa Rwandan genocide begins	The Channel Tunnel opens, connecting Britain and France O.J. Simpson arrested for double murder of his wife, Nicole Brown Simpson and her friend, Ron Goldman Lorena Bobbitt cuts off her husband's penis	**Forrest Gump** *Pulp Fiction* *Ed Wood* *Four Weddings and a Funeral* *Il Postino* *Natural Born Killers*	*True Lies* is the first $100 million film ever. It is nominated for 1 Academy Award.

1995

Ebola virus spreads in Zaire	O.J. Simpson trial for the murders of	**Braveheart** *Dead Man Walking* *Babe*	With his brother Michael, Cameron

History	Culture	Film Culture (Film titles in bold indicate Academy Award for best picture)	Cameron Biography
1995 (contined) Gas attack in Tokyo subway Oklahoma City bombing Yitzhak Rabin assassinated	his ex-wife and her friend (Simpson was an early candidate for Schwarzenegger's role in The Terminator)	Toy Story Clueless Underground Dead Man Apollo 13 Strange Days (story by James Cameron)	invents an underwater camera able to operate more than 12,000 feet below the ocean's surface. This camera is used to shoot the wreckage of the Titanic.
1996	Mad Cow Disease hits Britain Unabomber arrested	**The English Patient** Breaking the Waves Fargo Lone Star When We Were Kings Sling Blade Trainspotting Independence Day	Cameron co-directs T2 3D: Battle Across Time, an interactive Universal theme park attraction. Fox opens its Baja Studios, made especially for Titanic. It includes a 17-million gallon water tank, a 32,0000 square foot soundstage, and a 90 percent scale model of the Titanic.
1997 Hong Kong returned to China	Pathfinder sends back images of Mars Princess Diana dies in car crash Scientists clone sheep	**Titanic** The Sweet Hereafter Boogie Nights L.A. Confidential The Full Monty Good Will Hunting Men in Black	Cameron marries Linda Hamilton, star of The Terminator and Terminator 2. Titanic is the first $200 million film ever ($300

History	Culture	Film Culture	Cameron Biography
		(Film titles in bold indicate Academy Award for best picture)	
			including print and advertising costs). It is nominated for 14 Academy Awards. It wins 11, tying with *Ben Hur* for most Oscars won by a single film.
1998			
India and Pakistan test nuclear weapons U.S. President Clinton impeached	*Titanic* most successful movie ever Viagra on the market	**Shakespeare in Love** *Rushmore* *The Thin Red Line* *Out of Sight*	Cameron receives an honorary Doctor of Fine Arts from Carleton University, Ottawa, and an honorary degree from Ryerson University, Toronto.
1999			
The euro the new European Currency NATO attacks Serbia Panama Canal returned to Panama	Fear of Y2K bug JFK Jr. dies in plane accident	**American Beauty** *Being John Malkovich* *The Matrix* *Boys Don't Cry* *The Sixth Sense* *The Blair Witch Project*	Cameron divorces Linda Hamilton
2000			
George W. Bush wins contested U.S. presidential election; decided by Supreme Court (5–4)	Millennium fever	**Gladiator** *Memento* *Dancer in the Dark* *O Brother Where Art Thou* *Before Night Falls*	Cameron marries Suzi Amis, actor in *Titanic*. Cameron's TV series *Dark Angel* premieres.

RESOURCES

FILMOGRAPHY

Battle Angel (2009). Currently in pre-production at Twentieth Century Fox.

The Dive (2008). Currently in pre-production at Twentieth Century Fox.

Avatar (2008). Working title, *Project 880*, Currently in pre-production at Twentieth Century Fox.

Aliens of the Deep (2005)
>
> 47 min. Documentary. Buena Vista Pictures, Walt Disney Pictures
> Producers: James Cameron, Andrew Wight
> Directors: James Cameron, Steven Quale
> Cinematographer: Vince Pace
> Music: Jeehun Hwang

Ghosts of the Abyss (2003)
>
> 59 min. Documentary. Buena Vista Pictures, Walt Disney Pictures
> Producers: James Cameron, Chuck Comisky, Ed W. Marsh,
>   Gig Rackauskas, Janace Tashjian
> Director: James Cameron

Cinematographer: Vince Pace

Music: Joel McNeely

James Cameron's Expedition: Bismarck (2002)

120 min. TV

Producer: James Cameron

Directors: James Cameron, Gary Johnstone

Music: Jeehun Hwang

Dark Angel (2000–2002)

TV Series, Fox Television.

Creator, producer, writer: James Cameron

The Directors: James Cameron (1997)

60 min. Documentary. American Film Institute

Producer: Robert J. Emery

Director: Robert J. Emery

Titanic (1997)

194 min. Feature, Twentieth Century Fox, Paramount, Lightstorm
Entertainment

Producer: James Cameron

Director: James Cameron

Writer: James Cameron

Cinematographer: Russell Carpenter

Music: James Horner

Cast: Leonardo DiCaprio, Kate Winslet, Billy Zane, Frances Fisher,
Kathy Bates, Gloria Stuart, Bill Paxton

T2 3-D: Battle Across Time (1996)

12 min. Short feature

Producer: Chuck Comisky

Directors: James Cameron, John Bruno, Stan Winston

Cinematographers: Russell Carpenter, Russell J. Lyster

Music: Brad Fiedel

Cast: Arnold Schwarzenegger, Linda Hamilton, Robert Patrick,
Edward Furlong

Strange Days (1995)

> 145 min. Feature. Twentieth Century Fox
>
> Producer: James Cameron
>
> Director: Kathryn Bigelow
>
> Writers: James Cameron, Steven Charles Jaffe
>
> Cinematographer: Matthew Leonetti
>
> Music: Graeme Revel
>
> Cast: Ralph Fiennes, Angela Bassett, Juliette Lewis, Tom Sizemore,
> Michael Wincott

True Lies (1994)

> 141 min. Feature. Twentieth Century Fox
>
> Producers: James Cameron, Stephanie Austin
>
> Director: James Cameron
>
> Writer: James Cameron
>
> Cinematographer: Russell Carpenter
>
> Music: Brad Fiedel
>
> Cast: Arnold Schwarzenegger, Jamie Lee Curtis, Tom Arnold, Bill Paxton,
> Tia Carrere

Terminator 2: Judgment Day (1991)

> 139 min. Feature. Carolco Pictures, Lightstorm Entertainment, Pacific
> Western, Tri-Star
>
> Producers: James Cameron, Gale Anne Hurd
>
> Director: James Cameron
>
> Writers: James Cameron, William Wisher
>
> Cinematographer: Adam Greenberg
>
> Music: Brad Fiedel
>
> Cast: Arnold Schwarzenegger, Linda Hamilton, Robert Patrick,
> Edward Furlong

Point Break (1991)

> 117 min. Feature. Twentieth Century Fox, Tapestry Pictures
>
> Producerss: Peter Abrams, Robert L. Levy
>
> Director: Kathryn Bigelow

Writers: Kathryn Bigelow, James Cameron, W. Peter Iliff, Rick King

Cinematographer: Donald Peterman

Music: Mark Isham

Cast: Patrick Swayze, Keanu Reeves, Lori Petty, Gary Busey,
John C. McGinley

The Abyss (1989)

140 min. Feature. Twentieth Century Fox.

Producers: James Cameron, Gale Anne Hurd

Director: James Cameron

Writer: Chris Columbus

Cinematographers: Mikael Salomon, Dennis Skotak

Music: Alan Silvestri

Cast: Ed Harris, Mary Elizabeth Mastrantonio, Michael Biehn,
Leo Burmeister, Todd Graff

Aliens (1986)

138 min. Feature. Twentieth Century Fox, Brandywine.

Producer: Gale Anne Hurd

Director: James Cameron

Writer: James Cameron

Cinematographer: Adrian Biddle

Music: James Horner

Cast: Sigourney Weaver, Michael Biehn, Paul Reiser, Lance Henriksen,
Carrie Henn, Bill Paxton

Rambo: First Blood Part II (1986)

93 min. Feature. Tri-Star.

Producer: Buzz Feitshans

Director: George Pan Cosmatos

Writers: James Cameron, Kevin Jarre, Michael Kozol, Sylvester Stallone

Cinematographer: Jack Cardiff

Music: Jerry Goldsmith

Cast: Sylvester Stallone, Richard Crenna, Julia Nickson,
Charles Napier

The Terminator (1984)

    108 min. Feature. Hemdale, Orion, Pacific Western.

    Producer: Gale Anne Hurd

    Director: James Cameron

    Writers: James Cameron, William Wisher, Gale Anne Hurd

    Cinematographer: Adam Greenberg

    Music: Brad Fiedel

    Cast: Arnold Schwarzenegger, Linda Hamilton, Michael Biehn,
        Paul Winfield, Lance Henriksen

Piranha Part Two: The Spawning (1981)

    94 min. Feature. Saturn International Pictures.

    Producers: Jeff Schechtman, Chako Van Leeuwen,

    Director: James Cameron

    Writers: James Cameron, H.A. Milton, Lee Reynolds

    Cinematographer: Roberto d'Ettore Piazoli

    Music: Steve Powder

    Cast: Tricia O'Neil, Steve Marachuk, Lance Henriksen, Ricky G. Paull

Battle Beyond the Stars (1980)

    105 min. Feature. New World.

    Producers: Roger Corman, Ed Carlin

    Director: Jimmy T. Murakami

    Writer: John Sayles

    Cinematographer: Daniel Lacambre

    Art Directors: James Cameron, Charles William Breen

    Cast: Richard Thomas, George Peppard, Robert Vaughn, John Saxon,
        Darlanne Fluegel

NOTES

Chapter 1

1 Quoted in John H. Richardson, "Magnificent Obsession," *Premiere*, December 1997, p. 128.

2 Quoted in Marc Shapiro, *James Cameron: An Unauthorized Biography* (Los Angeles: Renaissance Books, 2000), p. 277.

3 For an account of the development of and debates touching auteur criticism, see *Theories of Authorship: A Reader*, John Caughie, ed. (London: Routledge and Kegan Paul, 1981).

4 *Titanic* was nominated for 14 awards (tying the record with *All about Eve*) and won 11, including best picture (tying the record with *Ben Hur*).

5 Shapiro, *James Cameron: An Unauthorized Biography*, p. 14.

6 *Titanic* has grossed over $1.8 billion in theaters worldwide, an additional $3.25 million in U.S. home rentals, and $900 million more in international rentals. James Horner's soundtrack for *Titanic* topped the charts for 16 weeks, and sold over 25 million units.

7 Brian D. Johnson, "Titanic Ambition: A Canadian sails Hollywood's high seas," *Maclean's*, vol. 110, no. 49, December 8, 1997, p. 86.

8 Cameron himself has often referred to it as his $200 million "chick flick."

9   *Titanic* is often compared to *Gone with the Wind* in its sweeping epic propor-
    tions, and to *Cleopatra* in its runaway expense, and Cameron himself has
    repeatedly drawn parallels between himself and *Dr. Zhivago* director David
    Lean. But in 1939 MGM carried the financial burden of *Gone with the Wind*
    on its own, and cooperated with another studio only to borrow Clark
    Gable from Columbia. In 1996, Fox and Paramount shared the tab for
    Titanic.

10 Thomas Doherty, "Genre, Gender and the *Aliens* Trilogy," in *The Dread of
    Difference* (Austin: University of Texas Press, 1996), Barry Keith Grant, ed.
    See Chapter 2 in this book.

11 Not only does he do the storyboards for most of his films, but he also
    sketched the portraits of Rose attributed to artist Jack Dawson (Leonardo
    DiCaprio) in *Titanic*.

12 Sean French, *The Terminator*, BFI Modern Classics Series (London: BFI
    Publishing, 1996), p. 9. *Esquire* magazine also selected it as its film of the
    1980s.

13 One wants to be careful about including *T3: Rise of the Machines* (2003) in
    this list since Cameron produced but did not write or direct it.
    Schwarzenegger is the best known but not the only actor with whom
    Cameron has worked repeatedly. Others include Michael Biehn (*The
    Terminator, Aliens*), Bill Paxton (*The Terminator, Aliens, Titanic*), and, of course,
    ex-wife Linda Hamilton (*The Terminator* series).

14 See, for example, Linda Hutcheon, *The Politics of Postmodernism* (New York:
    Routledge, 1989); Hal Foster, ed. *The Anti-Aesthetic: Essays on Postmodern Culture*
    (Port Townsend, Washington: Bay Press, 1983); Fredric Jameson,
    Postmodernism, or, the Cultural Logic of Late Capitalism (Durham, N.C.: Duke
    University Press, 1991).

15 In this Cameron's work shares something with actor/director Clint
    Eastwood's, whose films offer different social readings when seen as a
    group than when viewed as individual texts, the apparent vigilantism
    of *Dirty Harry* (1971) running up against the pro-union subtext of *Pale
    Rider* (1985). Though it was Don Siegel, not Eastwood, who directed *Dirty
    Harry*, it is certainly the film that, after a string of Sergio Leone Westerns
    in the 1960s, cemented his iconic status in the United States such that,

by the time he came to direct what he considered the anti-violence Western *Unforgiven* (1992), it was not least his portrayal of Harry Callahan that prevented the film from signifying that way to much of the audience. Cameron has also made cameo appearances in films (*The Muse*, 1999) and television series ("Entourage," 2005), but always plays himself.

16 Indeed, the debate about the nature of Cameron's female heroes and Cameron's status as a feminist director is one of the more sustained arguments about his work in academia. See Chapter 2 in this book.

17 Susan Jeffords, *Hard Bodies: Hollywood Masculinity in the Reagan Era* (New Brunswick: Rutgers University Press, 1994).

18 Jeffords astutely connects this to the assassination attempt on President Ronald Reagan. For another account of the relation between the attempted assassination and public culture, see Michael Paul Rogin, *Ronald Reagan, the Movie, and Other Episodes in Political Demonology* (Berkeley: University of California Press, 1987).

19 It is of no small interest that Dan O'Bannon's original script for *Alien* allowed for all of the characters to be cast with male or female actors.

20 This is a backstory left out of the original release version of the film, but which is restored in the director's cut. Its restoration only doubles Ripley's maternal motivations to action.

21 Amy Taubin, "The 'Alien' Trilogy from Feminism to Aids," in *Women and Film: A Sight and Sound Reader*, Pam Cook and Philip Dodd, eds. (Philadelphia: Temple University Press, 1993), pp. 93–96. Originally published in *Sight and Sound*, July 1992, vol. 2, number 3. See Chapter 2 in this book.

22 For more on this aspect of the maternal melodrama, see Robert Lang, "'I don't want to be like me ... but like the people in the Movie!': *Stella Dallas*" in *American Film Melodrama: Griffith, Vidor, Minelli* (Princeton, N.J.: Princeton University Press, 1989), pp. 132–52.

23 On the set of *Aliens*, Sigourney Weaver was critical of what she thought was the film's overuse of firearms and aspects of the script that were "extremely sexist." Shapiro, *Cameron: An Unauthorized Biography*, p. 145.

24 That the two Terminators sort into these readings is at least in part a historical accident. Financial constraints prevented Cameron from using the T-1000 in the first film as the original murderous cyborg. These constraints

also made it far easier to reorient the paradigm when Cameron met champion body builder Arnold Schwarzenegger, who originally auditioned for the role of Reese.

25 It is not without interest that for the third installment in the *Alien* series, *Alien*[3] (David Fincher, 1992), screenwriters David Giler, Walter Hill and Larry Ferguson immediately killed off Ripley's makeshift family, and then set the rest of the film at an all-male correctional facility at which there are, as Ripley incredulously states, "no weapons of any kind." Once her head is shaved and she resembles all the men in the prison, there is an androgynous gloss on the gender indeterminacy of the first *Alien*, as well as an allegorical engagement with the AIDS crisis, as Ripley's harboring of an alien within her own body can be understood. See Amy Taubin, "The 'Alien' Trilogy: from Feminism to AIDS," in *Women and Film: A Sight and Sound Reader*, eds. Pam Cook and Philip Dodd (Philadelphia: Temple University Press, 1993), pp. 93–100.

26 This feminist voice is not so difficult for Cameron to accord Rose, since the turn of the century of the film's plot is 100 years before the turn of the century of the film's release.

27 Cameron has never cast a typically beautiful female star in any of his films. Linda Hamilton, Sigourney Weaver, Mary Elizabeth Mastrantonio, Jamie Lee Curtis and Kate Winslet are, in a variety of ways, quite wide of the mark of what audiences seem to want in their Hollywood femininity – young, or recut and liposuctioned to look it, full of bosom, and yet rail thin everywhere else, delicately bobbed nose, and blonde, blonde, blonde.

28 The finale also clearly presages Cameron's most recent work on deep-sea life forms.

29 Jack's death is not the tragic ending for Rose that it first appears to be. It is a commonplace of feminist criticism of the film that Rose always knew that Jack would end up disappointing her in the end. As Katha Pollitt asked in *The Nation*, "How many happy artists' wives do you know?" Katha Pollitt, "Women and Children First," *The Nation* March 30, 1998, p. 9.

30 The family triad has an adjunct: the android Bishop (Lance Henrikson). As if to clarify that there is only one man in the house, human or otherwise,

the Alien Queen rips Bishop in half at the waist, effectively rendering him a eunuch, even though he never has the capacity for sexual action in the first place.

31 Johnson, p. 87.

32 See my treatment of Sharon Willis, *High Contrast: Race and Gender in Contemporary Hollywood Film* (Durham, N.C.: Duke University Press, 1997), especially chapter 3, "Combative Femininity: *Thelma and Louise* and *Terminator 2*," pp. 98–128, in Chapter 2 in this book.

33 A sequel to *True Lies* is reportedly being discussed, and that would bring the total to five.

34 Robert Burgoyne, *Film Nation: Hollywood Looks to U.S. History* (Minneapolis: University of Minnesota Press, 1997), p. 105. See also Alison Landsburg, "Prosthetic Memory: *Total Recall* and *Blade Runner*," *Body and Society*, nos. 3–4 (1995).

35 Indeed, in *Titanic*, Cameron seems to equate memory, even a fictitious one, with experience. As Cameron stand-in Bill Paxton's contemporary ocean explorer asks the older Rose (Gloria Stewart) in an early scene, "Are you ready to go back to Titanic?"

36 Considering Cameron's multiple wives: producer Gale Anne Hurd, director Kathryn Bigelow, actress Linda Hamilton, and unknown (to the industry) wife number one (Sharon Williams) – on whom Linda Hamilton's character Sarah Connor in *The Terminator* and *T2* was based – we must retool that old adage to say that, in Cameron's case, behind every great man there are several great women.

37 Not one to waste his training, Cameron's skills as an illustrator came in handy as he provided the sketches of Rose drawn by artist Jack Dawson (Leonardo DiCaprio).

38 If anything, the future of *Aliens* resonates with the American past of Vietnam, and Cameron was writing the scripts for this film and *Rambo: First Blood, Part 2* simultaneously. The *Rambo* script was almost completely revised by the film's star, Sylvester Stallone. Cameron's own assessment: "The action is mine, the politics are Stallone's." Quoted in Shapiro, *James Cameron: An Unauthorized Biography*, p. 136.

39 Anthony Lane, "The Shipping News: *Titanic* raises the Stakes of the Spectacular," *The New Yorker* December 15, 1997, 156–57.

40 Patricia Nelson Limerick, "Turnerians All," *American Historical Review*, vol. 100 (June 1995), p. 708. Italics in orginal.

41 It is a testament to the power of image over text in *Titanic*, as well as to the conventionality of Cameron's script, that, at the time, most people didn't seem to know he was quoting his own film on that night to remember.

42 Vivian Sobchack, "Bathos and Bathysphere: On Submersion, Longing and History in *Titanic*," in *Titanic: Anatomy of a Blockbuster*, Gaylyn Studlar and Kevin S. Sandler, eds. (New Brunswick, N.J.: Rutgers University Press, 1999), pp. 189–204.

43 "Going Back to Titanic: Interview with James Cameron," interview by Randall Frakes in *Titanic: James Cameron's Illustrated Screenplay*, annotated by Randall Frakes (New York: HarperCollins, 1998), p. xvii.

44 Ibid.

45 Guy Debord, *Society of the Spectacle* (Rebel Press, Aim Publications, 1987), paragraph 13. Originally published as *La Société du spectacle* (Paris: Editions Buchet-Chastel), 1967.

46 Thomas Schatz, "The New Hollywood," in *Film Theory Goes to the Movies*, Jim Collins, Hilary Radner and Ava Preacher Collins, eds. (New York: Routledge, 1993), pp. 9–10. Schatz's account of the blockbuster film is, while sometimes numbers driven to the exclusion of larger social phenomena, nevertheless exemplary.

47 Doubtless the folks on Madison Avenue tried just the same. Maybe they abandoned their efforts when they realized that nobody would want to supersize their Coke at McDonald's when that would mean getting an even bigger picture of the frozen Jack Dawson on the cup.

48 Source for USA www.the-numbers.com. Source for non-USA and international www.imdb.com. Figures not adjusted for inflation.

49 These numbers tell us something, but they don't tell us everything. They do tell us that, domestically, only a recent re-release of *Star Wars* accounts for why it holds second place as it does. But the

numbers don't tell us that, adjusted for inflation, *Gone with the Wind* (1939) is still the biggest moneymaker in United States history ($193 million actual/$863 million adjusted). The numbers also don't take into account the rising prices of tickets, or that some of these films (e.g., *Finding Nemo* and *The Lion King*) actually had far more viewers than the profits indicate, because so many of the tickets were sold at a reduced children's rate. The numbers also don't reflect the production costs of the films (making one film's $100 million or $200 million far more profitable than another's), specifying nothing about the rising costs of production as interest rates sky-rocketed in the 1970s and 1980s, or about the relatively low budgets of some of these films (*Home Alone*) at least as opposed to others (*Titanic*).

The numbers only begin to tell us who is responsible for these profits. Leading the older list are Steven Spielberg and George Lucas, who between them are responsible for six of the thirteen titles on the combined lists, and have earned a total of almost $3,389,000,000 (it really hits home when you see all the digits piling up like that). Cameron's total efforts are relatively more modest, but nevertheless gargantuan in the grand scheme of things: so far, *Titanic* has grossed $1.15 billion globally, $600 million domestically. *Terminator 2: Judgment Day* grossed $312 million globally and almost $205 million domestically (putting it at #3 globally, #23 domestically the year *Titanic* broke box-office records). *True Lies* grossed $219 million globally and $146 million domestically (making it #9 and #59, respectively that same year). Cameron's total grosses add up to almost $3 billion, not bad for only one King of the World. Almost half of that comes from *Titanic*. But on the newer list, while Spielberg and Lucas still rank high on the U.S. list, the international list now belongs as much to the *Harry Potter* and *Lord of the Rings* series.

50 *Tootsie's* U.S. gross was $177 million; *Good Will Hunting* grossed $138 million with a budget of $10 million; and internationally *The Full Monty* has grossed $200 million, with an additional $50 million in U.S. grosses on a budget of $3.5 million.

51   Those films are as follows:

	Release Date	Movie	Budget	U.S. Gross	Int'l Gross
1	5/4/2007	Spider-Man 3	$250m	unknown	unknown
2	6/30/2006	SuperMan Returns	$209m	unknown	unknown
3	12/14/2005	King Kong (2005)	$207m	$218,051,260	$547,051,260
4	6/30/2004	Spider-Man 2	$200m	$373,524,485	$783,924,485
5	12/19/1997	Titanic	$200m	$600,788,188	$1,835,400,000
6	7/28/1995	Waterworld	$175m	$88,246,220	$255,200,000
7	6/30/1999	Wild, Wild West	$175m	$113,805,681	$217,700,000
8	7/1/2003	T3: Rise of the Machines	$170m	$148,479,554	$366,800,000
9	11/10/2004	The Polar Express	$170m	$172,796,043	$296,596,043
10	5/7/2007	Van Helsing	$170m	$120,150,546	$269,150,546

Source: http://www.the-numbers.com/movies/records/budgets.html Budgets, box office and release dates for unreleased films are projected. Some films still in release at press time.

52   Anne Thompson, "Cameron's Way," *Premiere* August 1997, p. 63.
53   John H. Richardson, "Magnificent Obsession," *Premiere* December 1997, p. 125.
54   Ibid. p. 128.
55   Anne Thompson, "Cameron Is God," *Premiere* April 1998, p. 44.
56   Quoted in Robert J. Emery, *The Directors: Take One* (New York: Allworth Press, 2002), p. 136.
57   Benjamin Svetkey, "In the Wake of *Titanic*," *Entertainment Weekly* at http://www.ew.com/features/ 980206/titanic/index.html.
58   Andrew Essex, "Summer . . . What a Bummer," *Entertainment Weekly* (July 24, 1998), p. 22.
59   Ibid. p. 23.
60   See Sharon Waxman, "A Good, but Not Great Start for 'King Kong,'" *The New York Times*, December 19, 2005.
61   Lisa Schwatzbaum, "Monster's Ball: Peter Jackson's tragic, terrific *King Kong* is an old-school marvel worth celebrating," *Entertainment Weekly*, December 16, 2005, p. 58.
62   Quoted in Dan Bennet, "Low Key Movie Set Opens in Rosarito," *North Country Times* 7/1/01, http://www.nctimes.net/news/2001/20010701/65420.html
63   Audiences were happy to sit still, but the advertising for the film didn't presume that: in majors papers across the country the running time was listed at two hours and 74 minutes.

64   One may, in fact, pair the success of *Titanic* with any number of failures for slightly different reasons: *The Postman* because it was not only one of the biggest bombs of all time, but also because it was the bomb of the year the same year that *Titanic* set sail; *Cutthroat Island* (1995) because it really is the biggest bomb of all time, losing about $100 million.

65   We appear, at least in film culture, to be experiencing a second generation of postmodernism. If *Blade Runner* (1982) was both praised and lamented for its postmodern aesthetic – one that drew from myriad cultural and historical references apparently (and this I question) without any regard for actual history – films like Luc Besson's *The Fifth Element* (1997) take it one step further, constructing themselves intertextually through intertextual references to films (like *Blade Runner*) that are themselves almost wholly intertextual.

66   This is as far as I ought to go into such what iffing. Too many Titaniacs have done it more vividly than I ever could. Still, one may winkingly imagine that somewhere in Cameron's unused footage is a shot of the necklace sinking to the ocean floor and landing – plop! – next to the pair of handcuffs Jack wore.

67   See my discussion of Paul Virilio in Chapter 2 in this book.

68   Cameron's most recent directorial projects have been documentaries on the German battleship Bismarck (*James Cameron's Expedition: Bismarck* (2002), on the Titanic itself (*Ghosts of the Abyss*, 2003), and on deep-sea marine life (*Aliens of the Deep*, 2005). See filmography.

69   For an account of the misreporting see "Aquaman: Nearly Real for One Fleeting Cable News Moment," http://www.defamer.com/hollywood/media/aquaman-nearly-real-for-one-fleeting-cable-news-moment-186791. php which reports that the errors multiplied as the news copy misreported even the fictional grosses of *Aquaman*, which "in fact" totaled $116.8 million. Part of Cameron's agreement to participate in the fictional narrative of "Entourage" hinged on *Aquaman* opening big. See http://www.sfgate.com/cgi-bin/blogs/sfgate/detail?blogid=24&entry_id=7043

70   Lee's newest film, the bank heist thriller *Inside Man* (2006), is also explicit about its relation to 9/11, particularly the ways in which racism and ethnic tensions in New York City have rearranged themselves after the bombing of the towers.

71   In the Cameron-produced Steven Soderberg version of Stanislav Lem's

science fiction mystery *Solaris*, there is an opening sequence in which George Clooney's therapist, Dr. Kelvin, leads a group-therapy session in which members (including an Arab woman in a headscarf) talk about trauma, memory and media images, all of which are oblique, though certain, references to 9/11.

Chapter 2

1 Constance Penley, "Time Travel, Primal Scene and the Critical Dystopia" (on *The Terminator* and *La Jetée*), in *The Future of an Illusion: Film, Feminism, and Psychoanalysis* (Minneapolis: University of Minnesota Press, 1989), 121–39.

2 Penley cited a range of instances from even lower budget rip-offs like *Exterminator* to hard-core pornography (*The Sperminator*) to a rock band (*Terminators of Endearment*) to a Canadian journal (*The Manipulator*), p. 121.

3 Penley, p. 122.

4 Penley, p. 128.

5 Penley, pp. 129–31.

6 Penley, p. 131

7 Penley, p. 134.

8 Karen B. Mann, "Narrative Entanglements: *The Terminator*," *Film Quarterly*, vol. 43, no. 2, Winter 1989–90, pp. 17–27.

9 Mann, p. 17.

10 Mann, p. 19.

11 Mann, p. 20.

12 Mann, p. 25.

13 Susan Jeffords, *Hard Bodies: Hollywood Masculinity in the Reagan Era* (New Brunswick, NJ: Rutgers University Press, 1994).

14 See Jurgen Link, "Fanatics, Fundamentalists, Lunatics and Drug Traffickers – The New Southern Enemy Image," *Cultural Critique* 19 (Fall 1991), p. 35.

15 Jeffords, p. 25.

16 Jeffords, p. 163.

17 Jeffords, pp. 165, 170.

18   Jeffords, p. 173.

19   Stuart Hall, Dorothy Hobson, Andrew Lowe, and Paul Willis, *Culture, media, language: working papers in cultural studies, 1972–79* (Birmingham, West Midlands: Centre for Contemporary Cultural Studies, University of Birmingham, 1980); Simon During, ed. *The Cultural Studies Reader* (London: Routledge, 1993, reprinted 2001); Lawrence Grossberg, Cary Nelson, Paula Triechler, eds. *Cultural Studies* (London: Routledge, 1991).

20   Sharon Willis, *High Contrast: Race and Gender in Contemporary Hollywood Film* (Durham: Duke University Press, 1997), especially chapter 3, "Combative Femininity: *Thelma and Louise* and *Terminator 2*," pp. 98–128.

21   Willis, p. 8–9.

22   Willis, p. 21.

23   Willis, p. 126.

24   Robin Wood, "The Incoherent Text: Narrative in the 1970s," *Hollywood from Vietnam to Reagan . . .and Beyond* (New York: Columbia University Press, 2001), pp. 41–62, esp. p. 42.

25   Willis, p. 199–121.

26   Lisa Kennedy, "The Body in Question," in *Black Popular Culture*, a project by Michele Wallace, edited by Gina Dent (Seattle: Bay Press, 1992), 106–11.

27   Donald Bogle, *Toms, Coons, Mulattoes, Mammies & Bucks: An Interpretive History of Blacks in American Films* (New York: Bantam Books, 1974, revised and expanded, 2001.)

28   Kennedy, p. 107.

29   Kennedy, p. 107.

30   Kennedy, p. 109.

31   Kennedy, p. 109.

32   Doran Larson, "Machine as Messiah: Cyborgs, Morphs and the American Body Politic," *Cinema Journal*, vol. 36, no. 1, 1997, pp. 57–75.

33   Larson, p. 57.

34   John C. Kimball, "Machinery as Gospel Worker," *The Christian Examiner*, vol. 87 (November 1869), p. 327.

35   Larson, pp. 66–67.

36   Larson, p. 69.

37   John Berger, *Ways of Seeing* (London: Penguin Books, 1972), p. 143.

38   One essay that does is Teresa Rizzo, "The *Alien* Series: A Deleuzian Perspective," *Women: A Cultural Review*, vol. 15, no. 3, pp. 330–44.

39 Amy Taubin, "The 'Alien' Trilogy from Feminism to Aids," in *Women and Film: A Sight and Sound Reader*, Pam Cook and Philip Dodd, eds. (Philadelphia: Temple University Press, 1993), p. 93. Originally published in *Sight and Sound*, July 1992, vol. 2, number 3.

40 Taubin, pp. 94–96.

41 Franklin D. Gilliam, Jr., "The 'Welfare Queen' Experiment: How Viewers React to Images of African-American Mothers on Welfare," in *Nieman Reports*, vol. 53, no. 2, Summer 1999, p. 49.

42 For a systematic study of the impact of these images, see Gilliam, Jr.

43 Paul Virilio, "Aliens," in *Incorporations*, Jonathan Crary and Sanford Kwinter, eds. (New York: Zone/MIT Press, 1992), pp. 446–48. Translated by Brian Massumi.

44 Virilio, p. 449.

45 Thomas Doherty, "Genre, Gender and the *Aliens* Trilogy," in *The Dread of Difference*, Barry Keith Grant, ed., (Austin: University of Texas Press, 1996), p. 182.

46 Doherty, p. 189.

47 Doherty, pp. 191–92.

48 Doherty, p. 192.

49 Tim Blackmore, "'Is this Going to be Another Bug-Hunt?' S-F Tradition Versus Biology-as-destiny in James Cameron's *Aliens*," *Journal of Popular Culture*, vol. 29, no. 4, Spring 1996, pp. 211–26.

50 Blackmore, p. 211. The attacks in this essay can quite literally be that, and sometimes nearly *ad hominem*, or, more accurately, *ad feminam*, as Blackmore refers to the conclusions of a series of feminist interpretations of *Aliens* as "symptomatic of the slack quality of their close readings." (p. 212). This is obviously a subjective opinion, but this writer (in turn subjectively) finds Blackmore's readings to be no more taut, and often less.

51 Blackmore, p. 224.

52 Blackmore, p. 215.

53 Joe Abbott, "They Came from Beyond the Center: Ideology and Political Textuality in the Radical Science Fiction Films of James Cameron," *Literature Film Quarterly*, vol. 22, no. 1, 1994, pp. 21–27.

54 Abbott, p. 22.

55 Abbott, p. 22.

56   Abbott, p. 23.

57   Abbott, p. 26.

58   Louis Althusser, "Ideology and Ideological State Apparatuses," *Lenin and Philosophy and other Essays* (New York: Monthly review, 1971).

59   Robert Ray, *A Certain Tendency of the Hollywood Cinema, 1930–1980* (Princeton: Princeton University Press, 1985), p. 296.

60   James Kendrick, "Marxist Overtones in Three Films by James Cameron," *Journal of Popular Film and Television*, vol. 27, no. 3, Fall 1999, p. 38.

61   Kendrick, p. 39.

62   Kendrick, p. 40.

63   *Titanic* is most profitable in unadjusted dollars with a total domestic box office of $601 million. In adjusted dollars *Gone with the Wind* is the most profitable film of all time, with an adjusted box office of $1,293,085,600. None of these figures is completely verifiable, and rumors persisted that *Titanic's* budget was actually $285 million. Cameron disputed this in an interview in *Time* magazine, claiming it was actually $200 million. He continued: "This is the fourth time in a row that I have made a film that (rightly or wrongly) was called the most expensive film ever made. In any event, many of our favorite epics from the 30s, 40s and 50s would cost more than *Titanic* if made today." James Cameron, "Settling Accounts," *Time*, December 8, 1997, vol. 150, p. 92. Two days after *King Kong* opened it had made just $9.8 million, but this was before its first opening weekend, during which it grossed $50,130,145. On the welcome screen of America Online on Friday, December 16, 2005, a chat question asked members to weigh in on whether *King Kong* could beat *Titanic* at the box office. The response included the following:

> **Dishuponthestars:** not a chance . . . Titanic's record will never be broken. Wanna bet . . . even titanic's biggest fans agree that the movie's first half was beyond cheesy.
> **TheCoolerBlog:** I saw Kong already and I can tell you, NO cheese . . . and the movie broke my heart.
> **TheCoolerBlog:** it will outgross titanic
> **Dishuponthestars:** NO WAY . . . there's no rising star like Leo DiCaprio that women will go back to see again and again and again

Dishuponthestars: jack black's great, but he's no LEO

Dishuponthestars: adrian brody's great, but he's no LEO

Dishuponthestars: kong's cute, but he's no LEO

Ipingthere4iAM: and you know at least 1/4 of titanic's bottom line was teen girls going back to see LEO flash his beautiful blue eyes again.

Ipingthere4iAM: Plus, Kong doesn't have the Celine song

TheCoolerBlog: don't sing it

Ipingthere4iAM: MY HEART WILL GO ON . . . that song equals loads of tix sold . . .

Ipingthere4iAM: It brainwashed America.

Ipingthere4iAM: you know, the couple driving across town. then celine comes on the radio. and the car somehow winds up at the multiplex: TWO TICKETS for TITANIC please.

> Accessed on December 16, 2005 at http://journals.aol.com/
> thecoolerblog/AOLNewsCooler/#entry662

64 See for instance, *The Searchers: Essays and Reflections on John Ford's Classic Western*, Arthur Eckstein and Peter Lehman, eds. (Detroit: Wayne State University Press, 2004), and *Alfred Hitchcock's Rear Window* John Belton and Andrew Horton, eds. (Cambridge: Cambridge University Press, 2000). Even a volume on Spike Lee's *Do the Right Thing* was not published until eight years after the film's release: *Spike Lee's Do the Right Thing*, Mark Reid and Andrew Horton, eds. (Cambridge: Cambridge University Press, 1997). *The Matrix* (1999) saw a volume arrive three years after its release, as the second and third parts of the trilogy were rolling out in theaters (*The Matrix and Philosophy: Welcome to the Desert of the Real*, William Irwin, ed. (Peru, Illinois: Carus Publishing, 2002), and *The Lord of the Rings* trilogy also underwent rapid reconsideration with *The Lord of the Rings and Philosophy: One Book to Rule Them All*, Gregory Bassham and Eric Bronson, eds. (Peru, Illinois: Carus Publishing, 2003).

65 Gaylyn Studlar and Kevin S. Sandler, "The Seductive Waters of James Cameron's Film Phenomenon," Introduction to *Titanic: Anatomy of a Blockbuster*, Studlar and Sandler, eds. (New Brunswick, N.J.: Rutgers University Press, 1999), p. 4.

66   Studlar and Sandler, p. 6.

67   Peter Kramer, "Women First: 'Titanic' (1997), Action-Adventure Films and Hollywood's Female Audience," *Historical Journal of Film, Television and Radio*, vol. 18, no. 4, October 1998, pp. 599–619.

68   Kramer, p. 600.

69   Kramer, p. 605.

70   Kramer, p. 606.

71   Kramer, p. 607.

72   Katha Pollitt, "Subject to Debate: Women and Children First," *The Nation*, March 30, 1998, p. 9.

73   Pollitt, p. 9.

74   Pollitt, p. 9.

75   Pollitt, p. 9.

76   Robert von Dassanowsky, "A Mountain of a Ship: Locating the *Bergfilm* in James Cameron's *Titanic*," *Cinema Journal*, vol. 40, no. 4, Summer 2001, pp. 18–35. The major project of von Dassanowsky's essay is to establish the influence of the German *Bergfilm*, with its Weimar era gender politics and its careful balance of grand nature film and melodrama. His comparison of the Titanic and Princess Di phenomena is part of his rhetorical framing device of this exploration.

77   Von Dassanowsky, p. 18.

78   Von Dassanowsky, p. 27.

79   Von Dassanowsky, p. 20.

80   Von Dassanowsky, p. 33.

81   Todd F. Davis and Kenneth Womack, "Narrating the Ship of Dreams: The Ethics of Sentimentality in James Cameron's *Titanic*," *Journal of Popular Film and Television*, vol. 29, no. 1, Spring 2001, pp. 42–48.

82   Davis and Womack, p. 43.

83   Davis and Womack, p. 45.

84   See Fredric Jameson, "Postmodernism and Consumer Society," in *The Anti-Aesthetic: Essays on Postmodern Culture*, ed. Hal Foster (Port Townsend, WA: Bay Press, 1981), pp. 111–25.

85   James S. Hurley, "*Titanic* Allegories: the Blockbuster as Art Film," *Strategies*, vol. 14, no. 1, 2001, pp. 91–120.

86 Hurley, p. 93.

87 See Pierre Bourdieu, *The Field of Cultural Production* (New York: Columbia University Press, 1993).

88 Hurley, p. 97. Italics in original.

89 Quoted in Janet Maslin, "A Spectacle as Sweeping as the Sea," *The New York Times*, December 19, 1997.

90 Hurley, p. 110.

91 Hurley, p. 112.

92 Julian Stringer, "'The China Had Never Been Used!': On the Patina of Perfect Images in *Titanic*," in *Titanic: Anatomy of a Blockbuster*, Gaylyn Studlar and Kevin S. Sandler, eds. (New Brunswick, N.J.: Rutgers University Press, 1999), pp. 205–19. For another analysis of *Titanic* as a heritage film, see Fiona Terry-Chandler, "Vanished Circumstance: *Titanic*, Heritage, and Film," *International Journal of Heritage Studies*, vol. 6, no. 1, 2000, pp. 67–76.

93 Stringer, p. 206.

94 Stringer, p. 206.

95 Stringer, p. 210.

96 Stringer, p. 213.

97 See my "Size Does Matter: Notes on *Titanic* and James Cameron as Blockbuster *Auteur*," in *Titanic: Anatomy of a Blockbuster*, Gaylyn Studlar and Kevin S. Sandler, eds. (New Brunswick, N.J.: Rutgers University Press, 1999), pp. 132–54.

98 Vivian Sobchack, "Bathos and Bathysphere: On Submersion, Longing and History in *Titanic*," in *Titanic: Anatomy of a Blockbuster*, Gaylyn Studlar and Kevin S. Sandler, eds. (New Brunswick, N.J.: Rutgers University Press, 1999), pp. 189–204.

99 Sobchack, p. 191. Italics in original.

100 A.O. Scott, "Here's to Postwar America, We Never Really Knew Ye," *New York Times*, Sunday, December 4, 2004, Art & Leisure section, p. 24.

101 Sobchack, p. 194.

102 Sobchack, p. 202.

103 David Gerstner, "Unsinkable Masculinity: The Artist and the Work of Art in James Cameron's *Titanic*," *Cultural Critique* 50, Winter 2002, pp. 1–22.

104 "Camera-stylo," or "camera-pen," is a term coined by *Cahiers du Cinéma*

critic Alexandre Astruc to suggest that a film director was as capable of authoring a film as a novelist was a written work.

105 Gerstner, pp. 6–7.

106 Gerstner, pp. 10–12. Italics in original.

107 Gerstner, p. 15.

108 Kenneth Turan, "'Titanic' Sinks Again (Spectacularly)," *The Los Angeles Times*. December 19, 1997, p. 12.

109 Doug Dowling, "Critic Misses the Boat on Cameron's 'Titanic,'" *The Los Angeles Times*, December 27, 1997, p. 6.

110 David Courtney, "Critic Misses the Boat on Cameron's 'Titanic,'" p. 6.

111 Paul McElligott, "Critic Misses the Boat on Cameron's 'Titanic,'" p. 6.

112 *Titanic* won Golden Globe awards for Best Picture, Original Song, and Original Score, and James Cameron won for Best Director.

113 Kenneth Turan, "Oscars '98; You Try to Stop It; Make No Mistake about it, *Titanic*'s record-breaking success means bon voyage to the notion that a literate script is crucial to the filmmaking process," *The Los Angeles Times*, March 21, 1998, p. 1.

114 Turan, "Oscar's '98," p. 1.

115 Turan, Ibid.

116 James Cameron, "He's Mad as Hell at Turan; James Cameron Gets the Last Word on Our Critic's 'Titanic.' *The Los Angeles Times*, March 28, 1998, p. 1.

117 Cameron, Ibid.

118 Cameron, Ibid.

119 Cameron, Ibid.

120 Cameron, Ibid.

121 Monica Roman, "Fearless L.A. Times critic faces down King Cameron," *Variety*, vol. 370, no. 8, April 6, 1998, p. 4.

122 Quoted in David Kushner, "*Titanic* vs. Popotla," *Wired* August 7, 1998. Accessed on *Wired* web site, http://wired-vig.wired.com/news/culture/0,1284,14294,00.html

123 Accessed on the Rtmark web site, http://www.rtmark.com/legacy/popotla.html

124 Quoted in Kushner.

125 Fernando Larios Zepeda, Technical Commissioner for the Popotla

Fishermen association. The Association did not have the resources for professional English translation; this is their own. Full text accessible at http://www.rtmark.com/legacy/popotlaaustria.html

Chapter 3

1   Deregulation is hardly a complete explanation, but given the intimate relation between the second Bush administration and the corporations who are conducting the privately contracted side of the Second Gulf War, it is easy to see how the chickens have come home to roost, something hinted at in *Aliens*.

2   To be sure, Cameron occasionally offers the spectator the physical point of view of the alien drones as well. It is not so distorted that we cannot tell where they are and what they are doing, but it is just distorted – alien – enough that, unlike the Terminator's vision, it offers human sight less of what it wants to see, rather than more.

3   The only departure from this structure is when Ripley (and the viewer) needs to see a reaction shot from Hicks, which he cannot provide for himself. This is seen through Drake's camera.

4   The kind of heteronormative couple building that will also seem a compulsion in *The Abyss* extends beyond Ripley and Hicks. Vasquez, a female private who is coded as a lesbian, and Gorman, who has heretofore been seen as a bureaucratic panty waste, meet their redemptive and heroic end wrapped in each other's arms, setting off a sacrificial grenade just as they are swarmed by aliens.

5   Probably to do with the oppositional difference between screen left and camera left, the script has Ripley saying one direction, the actual film the other.

6   That a film with relatively populist, and leftist populist, readings of labor (e.g., Grunts) in the military and corporate system can still generate a seemingly right-wing affirmation of militarization is certainly not unique to *Aliens*, or to Cameron's work in general. Even a contemporary and unabashedly left-wing film like Stephen Gaghan's *Syriana* (2005) blunts its own critique – as Cameron does – by not giving any thought to how

industrial Hollywood filmmaking is as bound up in these discourses and problems as the actual objects of criticism.

7   "Interview with James Cameron," *Aliens*, Special Edition DVD, 1999. This interview also notes that principal designer Ron Cobb also suggested that Cameron was making a Vietnam War movie in outer space.

8   This is not the first direct quotation of 2001 in Cameron's work. Very early in *Aliens* there is a graphic match between the slope of Ripley's hypersleeping profile and the curvature of planet Earth. Its obviousness and its resonance seem intimately related to Stanley Kubrick's graphic match of the ape throwing up the bone that becomes the pen floating in zero gravity.

9   James Cameron and William Wisher, *Terminator 2: Judgment Day* (New York: Applause Books, 1991), pp. 39–46.

10 That this figure is Arab will produce a culturally biased film no amount of comedy can get out from under.

11 Or, to paraphrase the experimental filmmaker Hollis Frampton, when we say we wish to see more, we mean we wish to see less. ("So, if we do not like this particular film, we should not say: there is not enough here, I want to see more. We should say: there is too much here, I want to see less . . . So if we want to see what we call *more*, which is actually *less*, we must devise ways of subtracting and removing, one thing and another, more or less, from [the black screen,] our white rectangle.") Hollis Framtpon, "Lecture," in *The Avant-Garde Film: A Reader of Theory and Criticism*, P. Adams Sitney, ed. (New York: Anthology Film Archives, 1978), p. 276.

12 The terrorists are described as coming from "certain countries," none of whose members are anything but Arab, bringing a kind of latter-day Orientalism to *True Lies* – an Arab is an Arab is an Arab, and, with the exception of the Iranian (which in the context of the film is also to say Persian) Faisil, the token "good Arab," are as stereotypical as they come.

13 See Stanley Cavell, *Pursuits of Happiness: The Hollywood Comedy of Remarriage* (Cambridge: Harvard University Press, 1981).

14 Cameron does not see *Titanic* as inconsistent with his other films. "After *Titanic* came out, everybody acted like it was a big surprise that I had done a love story. Well, *The Terminator* was a love story. *The Abyss*, also, definitely

was, and to a lesser degree, so was *Aliens*. A mother-daughter love story." Quoted in Paul M. Sammon, "Mothers with Guns," the introduction to *Aliens: The Illustrated Screenplay* by James Cameron, foreword by James Cameron (London: Orion Books, 2001), p. 18.

15 "Going Back to Titanic: Interview with James Cameron," interview by Randall Frakes in *Titanic: James Cameron's Illustrated Screenplay*, annotated by Randall Frakes (New York: HarperCollins, 1998), p. ix.

16 Cameron had listened to Enya while he wrote *Titanic*, and wanted her to write the score. When she would not he turned to James Horner, who had written his *Aliens* score, and asked him to write something that sounded like Enya.

17 This shot will be seen in its original full color form almost half an hour later in the embarkation scene. If the finding of an object is really the refinding of an object, Cameron's cameo might be far easier to spot here.

18 Rose has had one other flash-cut memory before this. Upon seeing her drawing for the first time in 84 years, she suddenly recalls images of Jack Dawson's hand sketching (Dawson is played by Leonardo DiCaprio, but the hand pictured is in fact Cameron's), and a Sergio Leone-esque close-up of DiCaprio's intensely probing eyes.

BIBLIOGRAPHY

Abbott, Joe, "They Came from Beyond the Center: Ideology and Political Textuality in the Radical Science Fiction Films of James Cameron," in *Literature Film Quarterly*, vol. 22, no. 1, 1994, pp. 21–27.

Bernstein, Matthew, "'Floating Triumphantly': The American Critics on *Titanic*," in *Titanic: Anatomy of a Blockbuster*, Gaylyn Studlar and Kevin S. Sandler, eds. (New Brunswick, N.J.: Rutgers University Press, 1999), pp. 14–28.

Bernstein, Rhona, "Mommie Dearest: *Aliens, Rosemary's Baby* and Mothering," *Journal of Popular Culture*, vol. 24, no. 2 (1990), pp. 55–73.

Blackmore, Tim, "'Is this Going to be Another Bug-Hunt?' S-F Tradition Versus Biology-as-destiny in James Cameron's *Aliens*," in *Journal of Popular Culture*, vol. 29, no. 4, Spring 1996, pp. 211–26.

Cameron, James, "Settling Accounts," *Time*, December 8, 1997, vol. 150, p. 92.

—— *Titanic: James Cameron's Illustrated Screenplay*, annotated by Randall Frakes (New York: HarperCollins, 1998).

—— "He's Mad as Hell at Turan; James Cameron Gets the Last Word on Our Critic's 'Titanic.' *The Los Angeles Times*, March 28, 1998, p. 1.

Cameron, James and William Wisher, *Terminator 2: Judgment Day*, illustrated screenplay (New York: Applause Books, 1991).

Curtis, Bryan, "James Cameron: Will the Titanic director ever resurface?" Slate.com, February 2, 2005, http://www.slate.com/id/2113046/.

von Dassanowsky, Robert, "A Mountain of a Ship: Locating the *Bergfilm* in James Cameron's *Titanic*," *Cinema Journal*, vol. 40, no. 4, Summer 2001, pp. 18–35.

Davis, Todd F. and Kenneth Womack, "Narrating the Ship of Dreams: The Ethics of Sentimentality in James Cameron's *Titanic*," *Journal of Popular Film and Television*, vol. 29, no. 1, Spring 2001, pp. 42–48.

Doherty, Thomas, "Genre, Gender and the *Aliens* Trilogy," in *The Dread of Difference* Barry Keith Grant, ed. (Austin: University of Texas Press, 1996), pp. 181–199.

Emery, Robert, "The Films of James Cameron," in *The Directors: Take One* (New York: Allworth Press, 2002), pp. 113–39.

Frakes, Randall, "Going Back to Titanic: Interview with James Cameron," in *Titanic: James Cameron's Illustrated Screenplay*, annotated by Randall Frakes (New York: HarperCollins, 1998).

French, Sean, *The Terminator*, BFI Modern Classics Series (London: BFI Publishing, 1996).

Gabbard, Krin, "*Aliens* and the New Family Romance." *Post Script: Essays in Film and the Humanities* vol. 8, no. 1, 1988, pp. 29–42.

Grady, Frank, "Arnoldian Humanism, or Amnesia and Autobiography in the Schwarzenegger Action Film," *Cinema Journal*, vol. 42, no. 2, Winter 2003, pp. 41–56.

Greenberg, Harvey, "Fembo: *Aliens*' Intentions," *Journal of Popular Film and Television*, vol. 15, no. 4, Winter 1988, pp.1 64–71.

Griffin, Nancy, "James Cameron Is the Scariest Man in Hollywood," *Esquire*, December 1997, 98–104.

Heard, Christopher, *Dreaming Aloud: The Life and Films of James Cameron* (Toronto: Doubleday Canada, 1997; revised edition, 1998) Introduction by Roger Corman.

Hurley, James S., "*Titanic* Allegories: the Blockbuster as Art Film," *Strategies*, vol. 14, no. 1, 2001, pp. 91–120.

Jancovich, Mark, "Modernity and Subjectivity in the *Terminator*: The Machine as Monster in Contemporary American Culture," *The Velvet Light Trap*, no. 30, Fall, 1992, pp. 3–18.

Jeffords, Susan, "Can Masculinity Be Terminated?" in *Screening the Male: Exploring Masculinities in Hollywood Cinema*, Steven Cohan and Ina Rae Hark eds. (London: Routledge, 1993), pp. 245–62.

——— *Hard Bodies: Hollywood Masculinity in the Reagan Era* (New Brunswick, N.J.: Rutgers University Press, 1994).

Jennings, Ros, "Desire and Design: Ripley Undressed," in *Immortal, Invisible: Lesbians and the Moving Image*, Tamsin Wilton, ed. (London: Routledge, 1995), pp. 193–206.

Keller, Alexandra, "Size Does Matter: Notes on *Titanic* and James Cameron as Blockbuster *Auteur*," in *Titanic: Anatomy of a Blockbuster*, Gaylyn Studlar and Kevin S. Sandler, eds. (New Brunswick, N.J.: Rutgers University Press, 1999), pp. 132–54.

Kendrick, James, "Marxist Overtones in Three Films by James Cameron," *Journal of Popular Film and Television*, vol. 27, no. 3, Fall 1999, p. 38.

Kennedy, Lisa, "The Body in Question," in *Black Popular Culture*, a project by Michele Wallace, edited by Gina Dent (Seattle: Bay Press, 1992), pp. 106–11.

Kramer, Peter, "Women First: 'Titanic' (1997), Action-Adventure Films and Hollywood's Female Audience," *Historical Journal of Film, Television and Radio*, vol. 18, no. 4, October 1998, pp. 599–619. Reprinted in *Titanic: Anatomy of a Blockbuster*.

Kushner, David, "Titanic vs. Popotla," *Wired*, August 7, 1998. Accessed on *Wired* web site, http://wired-vig.wired.com/news/culture/0,1284, 14294,00.html

Larios, Fernando Zepeda, Technical Commissioner for the Popotla Fishermen Association. Full text accessible at http://www.rtmark.com/legacy/ popotlaaustria.html

Larson, Doran, "Machine as Messiah: Cyborgs, Morphs and the American Body Politic," *Cinema Journal*, vol. 36, no. 1, 1997, pp. 57–75.

Lehman, Peter and Susan Hunt, "'Something and Someone Else': The Mind, the Body and Sexuality in *Titanic*," in *Titanic: Anatomy of a Blockbuster*, Gaylyn Studlar and Kevin S. Sandler, eds. (New Brunswick, NJ: Rutgers University Press, 1999), pp. 89–107.

Lubin, David M., *Titanic*, BFI Modern Classics Series (London: BFI Publishing, 1999).

Mann, Karen B., "Narrative Entanglements: *The Terminator*," *Film Quarterly*, vol. 43, no. 2, Winter 1989–90, pp. 17–27.

Maslin, Janet, "A Spectacle as Sweeping as the Sea," *The New York Times*, December 19, 1997.

Massey, Anne and Mike Hammond, "'It Was True! How Can You Laugh?': History and Memory in the Reception of *Titanic* in Britain and Southampton," in *Titanic: Anatomy of a Blockbuster*, Gaylyn Studlar and Kevin S. Sandler, eds. (New Brunswick, N.J.: Rutgers University Press, 1999), pp. 239–64.

Middleton, Peter and Tim Woods, "Textual Memory: the Making of the *Titanic*'s Literary Archive," *Textual Practice*, vol. 15, no. 3, 2001, pp. 507–26.

Miles, Geoff and Carol Moore, "Explorations, Prosthetics and Sacrifice: Phantasies of the Maternal Body in the *Alien* Trilogy," *CineAction!*, vol. 30, 1992, pp. 54–62.

Munich, Adrienne and Maura Spiegel, "Heart of the Ocean: Diamonds and Democratic Desire in *Titanic*," in *Titanic: Anatomy of a Blockbuster*, Gaylyn Studlar and Kevin S. Sandler, eds. (New Brunswick, N.J.: Rutgers University Press, 1999), pp. 155–68.

Nash, Melanie and Martti Lahti, "'Almost Ashamed to Say I am One of Those Girls': *Titanic*, Leonardo DiCaprio, and the Paradoxes of Girls' Fandom," in *Titanic: Anatomy of a Blockbuster*, Gaylyn Studlar and Kevin S. Sandler, eds. (New Brunswick, N.J.: Rutgers University Press, 1999), pp. 64–88.

Negra, Diane, "*Titanic*, Survivalism, and the Millennial Myth," in *Titanic: Anatomy of a Blockbuster*, Gaylyn Studlar and Kevin S. Sandler, eds. (New Brunswick, N.J.: Rutgers University Press, 1999), pp. 220–38.

Ouellette, Laurie, "Ship of Dreams: Cross-Class Romance and the Cultural Fantasy of *Titanic*," in *Titanic: Anatomy of a Blockbuster*, Gaylyn Studlar and Kevin S. Sandler, eds. (New Brunswick, N.J.: Rutgers University Press, 1999), pp. 169–88.

Parisi, Paula, *Titanic and the Making of James Cameron* (New York: New Market Press, 1998).

Penley, Constance, "Time Travel, Primal Scene and the Critical Dystopia (on *The Terminator* and *La Jetée*), in *The Future of an Illusion: Film, Feminism, and Psychoanalysis* (Minneapolis: University of Minnesota Press, 1989), pp. 121–39.

Pfiel, Fred, "Home Fires Burning: Family Noir in *Blue Velvet* and *Terminator 2*," in *Shades of Noir*, Joan Copjec, ed. (London: Verso, 1993), pp. 227–59.

Pollitt, Katha, "Subject to Debate: Women and Children First," *The Nation*, March 30, 1998, p. 9.

Rizzo, Teresa, "The *Alien* Series: A Deleuzian Perspective," *Women: A Cultural Review*, vol. 15, no. 3, pp. 330–44.

Rushing Hocker, Janice, "Evolution of 'the New Frontier' in *Alien* and *Aliens*: Patriarchal Co-Optation of the Feminine Archetype," *Quarterly Journal of Speech*, vol. 75, no. 1, 1989, pp. 1–24.

Shapiro, Marc, *James Cameron: An Unauthorized Biography of the Filmmaker* (Los Angeles: Renaissance Books, 2000).

Slattery, Dennis Patrick, "Demeter Persephone and the *Alien*(s) Cultural Body," *New Orleans Review*, vol. 19, no. 1, 1992, pp. 30–35.

Smith, Jeff, "Selling My Heart: Music and Cross-Promotion in *Titanic*," in *Titanic: Anatomy of a Blockbuster*, Gaylyn Studlar and Kevin S. Sandler, eds. (New Brunswick, N.J.: Rutgers University Press, 1999), pp. 46–63.

Sobchack, Vivian, "Bathos and Bathysphere: On Submersion, Longing and History in *Titanic*," in *Titanic: Anatomy of a Blockbuster*, Gaylyn Studlar and Kevin S. Sandler, eds. (New Brunswick, N.J.: Rutgers University Press, 1999), pp. 189–204.

Stringer, Julian, "'The China Had Never Been Used!': On the Patina of Perfect Images in *Titanic*," in *Titanic: Anatomy of a Blockbuster*, Gaylyn Studlar and Kevin S. Sandler, eds. (New Brunswick, N.J.: Rutgers University Press, 1999), pp. 205–19.

Studlar, Gaylyn and Kevin S. Sandler, "The Seductive Waters of James Cameron's Film Phenomenon," Introduction to *Titanic: Anatomy of a Blockbuster*, Studlar and Sandler, eds. (New Brunswick, N.J.: Rutgers University Press, 1999), pp. 1–13.

Taubin, Amy, "The 'Alien' Trilogy from Feminism to Aids," in *Women and Film: A Sight and Sound Reader*, Pam Cook and Philip Dodd, eds. (Philadelphia: Temple UP, 1993), pp. 93–96. Originally published in *Sight and Sound*, vol. 2, number 3, July 1992.

Telotte, J.P., "*The Terminator, Terminator 2*, and the Exposed Body," *Journal of Popular Film and Television*, vol. 20, no. 2, Summer 1992, pp. 26–35.

Terry-Chandler, Fiona, "Vanished Circumstance: *Titanic*, Heritage, and Film," *International Journal of Heritage Studies*, vol. 6, no. 1, 2000, pp. 67–76.

Turan, Kenneth, "'Titanic' Sinks Again (Spectacularly)," *The Los Angeles Times*, December 19, 1997, p. 12.

—— "Oscars '98; You Try to Stop It; Make No Mistake about it, *Titanic's* record-breaking success means bon voyage to the notion that a literate script is crucial to the filmmaking process," *The Los Angeles Times*, March 21, 1998, p. 1.

Vaughn, Thomas, "Voices of Sexual Distortion: Rape, Birth, and Self Annihilation Metaphors in the *Aliens* Trilogy," *Quarterly Journal of Speech*, vol. 81, no. 4, 1995, pp. 423–35.

Virilio, Paul, "Aliens," in *Incorporations*, Jonathan Crary and Sanford Kwinter, eds. (New York: Zone/MIT Press, 1992), pp. 446–48. Translated by Brian Massumi.

Weil, Andrew, "James Cameron on Battle Angel!," interview with James Cameron, January 10, 2005, http://www.comingsoon.net/news/top-news.php?id = 7877.

Willis, Sharon, *High Contrast: Race and Gender in Contemporary Hollywood Film* (Durham, N.C.: Duke University Press, 1997), especially chapter 3, "Combative Femininity: *Thelma and Louise* and *Terminator 2*," pp. 98–128.

Wyatt, Justin and Katherine Vlesmas, "The Drama of Recoupment: On the Mass Media Negotiation of *Titanic*," in *Titanic: Anatomy of a Blockbuster*, Gaylyn Studlar and Kevin S. Sandler, eds. (New Brunswick, N.J.: Rutgers University Press, 1999), pp. 29–45.

Useful Websites

http://www.students.uni-mainz.de/manng001/spezial/cameron_chat.htm Transcript of MSN Online Tonight with James Cameron (conducted January 21, 1998).

Bryan Curtis, "James Cameron: Will the Titanic director ever resurface?" Slate.com, February 2, 2005, http://www.slate.com/id/2113046/.

Andrew Weil, "James Cameron on Battle Angel!," interview with James Cameron, January 10, 2005, http://www.comingsoon.net/news/top-news.php?id = 7877.

http://www.d2.com Official web site for James Cameron's special effects company.

http://www.titanicmovie.com/us/home.html Official web site for *Titanic*.
Includes interviews, production notes, virtual ship tours, and more.

Unofficial *Terminator* fan site: http://members.aol.com/wormpix/term.html

Unofficial *Alien* series fan site: http://www.planetavp.com/amr/html/links/
linkss.html#loffi includes comprehensive list of links to other sites.

Other official sites, links below, for Cameron's films have less useful content.
Not every film has an official website.

The Terminator www.sonypictures.com

Aliens www.foxhome.com/alienlegacy

The Abyss www.abyssdvd.com

For links to other websites, see www.imdb.com and www.allmovieguide.com.

INDEX

NOTE: Page numbers in italics indicate an illustration. Where information is in a note, the note number follows the page number.

GENRE AND HOLLYWOOD

STEVE NEALE

Genre and Hollywood provides a comprehensive introduction to the study of genre. In this important new book, Steve Neale discusses all the major concepts, theories and accounts of Hollywood and genre, as well as the key genres which theorists have written about, from horror to the Western. He also puts forward new arguments about the importance of genre in understanding Hollywood cinema.

Neale takes issue with much genre criticism and genre theory, which has provided only a partial and misleading account of Hollywood's output. He calls for broader and more flexible conceptions of genre and genres, for more attention to be paid to the discourses and practices of Hollywood itself, for the nature and range of Hollywood's films to be looked at in more detail, and for any assessment of the social and cultural significance of Hollywood's genres to take account of industrial factors.

In detailed, revisionist accounts of two major genres - film noir and melodrama - Neale argues that genre remains an important and productive means of thinking about both New and old Hollywood, its history, its audiences and its films.

ISBN10: 0-415-026059 (hbk)
ISBN10: 0-415-026067 (pbk)

ISBN13: 978-0-415-026055 (hbk)
ISBN13: 978-0-415-026062 (pbk)

THE FILM CULTURES READER

EDITED BY GRAEME TURNER

This companion reader to *Film as Social Practice* brings together key writings on contemporary cinema, exploring film as a social and cultural phenomenon.

Key features of the reader include:

* thematic sections, each with an introduction by the editor
* a general introduction by Graeme Turner
* sections: understanding film, film technology, film industries, meanings and pleasures, identities, audiences and consumption

Contributors include: Tino Balio, Sabrina Barton, Tony Bennett, Jacqueline Bobo, Edward Buscombe, Stella Bruzzi, Jim Collins, Barbara Creed, Richard Dyer, Jane Feuer, Miriam Hansen, John Hill, Marc Jancovich, Susan Jeffords, Isaac Julien, Annette Kuhn, P. David Marshall, Judith Mayne, Kobena Mercer, Tania Modleski, Steve Neale, Tom O'Regan, Stephen Prince, Thomas Schatz, Gianluca Sergi, Ella Shohat, Jackie Stacey, Janet Staiger, Robert Stam, Chris Straayer, Yvonne Tasker, Stephen Teo, Janet Wollacott, Justin Wyatt.

ISBN10: 0-415-25281-4 (hbk)
ISBN10: 0-415-25282-2 (pbk)

ISBN13: 978-0-415-25281-2 (hbk)
ISBN13: 978-0-415-25282-9 (pbk)

RELATED TITLES FROM ROUTLEDGE

MOVIE MUSIC, THE *FILM* READER

EDITED BY KAY DICKINSON

From silent film accompaniment and classical films scores to jazz, rock 'n' roll movies and pop soundtracks, Movie Music, the Film Reader argues for a broader understanding of the roles of music in films, bringing together key articles on subjects such as rockumentary, fandom and animation.

Movie Music, the Film Reader is divided into four sections, each with an introduction by the editor:

- The place of the song
- The formal politics of music on film
- The meanings of the film score,
- Crossing over into the narrative.

Contributors include: Theodore Adorno, Philip Brophy, Kay Dickinson, Hans Eisler, Claudia Gorbman, Lawrence Grossberg, Kathryn Kalinak, Keir Keightley, Lisa Lewis, Carl Plantinga, Jeff Smith, and Anastasia Valassopoulos.

ISBN10: 0-415-28159-8 (hbk)
ISBN10: 0-415-28160-1 (pbk)

ISBN13: 978-0-415-28159-1 (hbk)
ISBN13: 978-0-415-28160-7 (hbk)

Available at all good bookshops
For ordering and further information please visit:
www.routledge.com